THE BORDER

In the Sprucewoods

The Border

Foreword by
His Grace the Duke of Buccleuch and Queensberry,
K.T., G.C.V.O.
and
His Grace the Duke of Northumberland, K.G.

Edited by
JOHN WALTON, D.Sc., Sc.D., LL.D., F.R.S.E.
Regius Professor of Botany in the University of Glasgow
Forestry Commissioner 1949-1954

LONDON
HER MAJESTY'S STATIONERY OFFICE
1962

First Edition 1958
Second Edition 1962

FOREWORD

Those of us who had watched the planting, growth and development of the Forests of Kielder, Wark, Redesdale, Kershope, Newcastleton and Wauchope during the last forty years, welcomed the decision of the Forestry Commission to establish in this lovely and historic area of the Scottish Border another Forest Park.

Large blocks of forest are comparatively rare in the British Isles, and are likely to remain so owing to our limited acreage and the widely recognised need for the closest integration of agriculture and forestry.

The area covered by this guide has, therefore, a special interest and we feel sure that the facilities now afforded by the Forestry Commission will provide the public with opportunity for wide enjoyment and recreation.

The contributors to this book are to be congratulated on giving us so much interesting and easily assimilated material to read. In a guide book such as this the articles must of necessity be condensed but we hope that they will serve to stimulate readers—whether they be historians, botanists, geologists or just the travellers who find happiness in the open countryside—to visit the Park and seek further for themselves the beautiful scenery and historic places they will find there.

From Roman times, through the Saxon, Danish and Norman periods, throughout the Middle Ages and until the Union of England and Scotland the Border played a conspicuous part in our national history and during the wars between England and Scotland was the scene of periodic warfare and almost continuous raids.

A great deal has been written about the stirring history of those latter times by Sir Walter Scott and other authors and much romance and legend still remains, of which perhaps the Ballad of Chevy Chase is the best known. It was of this poem that Sir Phillip Sidney wrote in his *Defence of Poetry*: 'I never heard that old song of Percy and Douglas, that I found not my heart moved more than with a trumpet; and yet it is sung but by some blinde crowder, with no rougher voice than rude style; which being so evil apparelled in the dust and cobweb of that uncivill age, what would it work, trimmed in the gorgeous eloquence of Pindare.'

Now the area is given over to the peaceful pursuits of husbandry and forestry; but it should be remembered that the community of interests of the local inhabitants, which is very strong in hill areas, has its roots in a long past and upbringing in that environment.

The facilities provided by the Forestry Commission in this extensive area place an obligation on visitors to have an understanding of and consideration for those who live and work there. Enormous damage can be done to agriculture by the few careless visitors who walk over crops, break down walls or leave gates open; and to forestry by those who fail to comply with the minimum necessary restrictions and regulations that the Commission must make in order to protect the forests, and especially the young plantations, from damage—particularly by fire.

We hope that with this book as a guide many generations will find happiness, recreation and interest in the Border Forest Park.

Buccleuch and Queensberry
Northumberland

CONTENTS

v

ACKNOWLEDGMENTS

In addition to the authors whose names appear elsewhere, the following contributors have kindly assisted with the production of this Guide:—

Drawings. The cover picture and the frontispiece are from boxwood engravings by Mr. George Mackley, who also did the drawing for the chapter on Vegetation.

Miss Joan Hassall drew the chapter heading for Wild Animal Life.

The remaining chapter headings were prepared by Mr. Clixby Watson, after sketches by the late Cecile Walton.

The endpapers are by Mr. Charles Howarth.

Photographs. Nearly all the photographs which illustrate this Guide were kindly provided by Mr. Valdemars Blankenburgs, a Forestry Commission surveyor at Kielder Forest.

The exceptions, to which thanks are due to the people named, are: The Roman Wall by Messrs. Fox Photos., Ledmore Lining-out Plough by Mr. J. M. Hood, Crag Lough by Dr. W. A. Clark and Shorteared Owl by Mr. H. R. Lowes, and the view of the North Tyne Valley by Mr. Geoffrey N. Wright.

Maps. All the topographical maps are based on the Ordnance Survey, by permission of the Director General, Ordnance Survey.

The sketch map of the region, following page 64, has been prepared by Studio Corot, London, and the remaining topographical maps are by Mr. Marc Sale of Hampton, Middlesex.

The geological map was provided by Dr. G. A. L. Johnson, and is based, by permission of the Director General, Geological Survey and Museum, on the work of H. M. Geological Survey.

Poetry. We are indebted to Messrs. Faber and Faber for permission to use the lines on page 75, by Marion Angus; and to Messrs. Meiklejohn and Son, Ltd., for permission to quote those on pages 18 and 39, by Will H. Ogilvie.

General. Thanks are also due to the members of the Forestry Commission staff who are concerned with the administration of the Border Forests. Their exhaustive local knowledge has proved of great assistance in the compilation of this Guide.

We travelled in the print of olden wars;
Yet all the land was green,
And love we found and peace
Where fire and war had been.
—W. P. Bannatyne

INTRODUCTION

BY PROFESSOR JOHN WALTON

There are now seven National Forest Parks established by the Forestry Commission in Britain and each has its special features of interest and beauty. This, the Border Park, is the most recently formed, having been declared as recently as 1955, and it is notable for several reasons. It contains the largest planted forest in Britain and bears witness to the very important work which is being undertaken by the Forestry Commission to establish forests which will supply the nation with a substantial source of timber. The area which has been afforested was principally hill land of low agricultural value which supported but few grazing animals. Its use for forestry has been agreed with the respective Agricultural Department on each side of the Border.

The establishment of these forests has already led to an increase in the population of the district, an increase which will be progressive as the forests mature and local crafts and industries related to forestry develop. Thus we look forward to this sparsely populated land developing into an active and prosperous rural area.

Those who enjoy the countryside will find here plenty of interesting walks in the wide park area where there is fine scenery and many interesting historical relics. There is also wide scope for those interested in natural history. The Forestry Commission welcomes visitors and trusts that it will get their co-operation in preserving

1

what is interesting and beautiful, but above all in helping to ensure that there is no risk of fire. In this enormous area of young plantations fire is a real menace and incalculable damage might be done by a carelessly dropped match or cigarette end.

I acknowledge with gratitude the co-operation which has been so willingly given in the production of this book by those who have contributed the chapters which follow and in which the reader will find a wide range of interests.

My special thanks are due to Mr. Herbert Edlin who has been responsible for the major part of the work in preparing the book for publication and who throughout has been a most enthusiastic and helpful colleague.

Thanks are also due to those who have assisted in the illustration of this book, and whole names appear on the acknowledgments page.

Whiles in the silence o' the nicht,
  bedded amang the withered ferns,
I lie an' watch auld Border reivers
  rise frae beneath their funeral cairns,
An' ride ahint their limpin' drove,
  while faur awa' ayont the moss
The rid glare o' the blazin' thatch
  tells o' some English yeoman's loss,
So they ride by, their spears in rest,
  their armour glintin' in the mune
An' vanish when the nicht is dune
                              The Drover—C. J. Kirk

THE LAND AND THE PEOPLE
BY H. L. EDLIN

When, early in the present century, afforestation was begun in the
Borders, they formed one of the loneliest and least developed regions
of Britain. Our object here is to speculate—since few written
records remain—on the factors which led to so large a stretch of
land remaining so thinly peopled, and to see what changes will
follow the coming of modern forests on a grand scale. The works
of students of geology, vegetation, ecology, archaeology, and history
combine to throw a good deal of light on the past of this fascinating
region.

VANISHED FORESTS

The geological record shows that the Ice Age glaciers left the
sandstones, shales, and limestones of the Border hills deeply buried
below a thick deposit of Boulder Clay, impervious to water, over
which burns meandered downhill in various directions to join the
North Tyne, the Rede, the Liddel, the Jed, or the Rule Water.
Where drainage was poor, thick beds of peat developed. As

3

explained by Dr. Clark in the chapter on the vegetation, this peat preserves the pollen grains of trees and plants so well that their species can be identified, and in this way a picture can be built up of the primeval forests that gradually spread over the hill slopes in prehistoric times. Birch, alder, oak, rowan, Scots pine, elm, lime and hazel appear in the pollen deposits, which have been examined by Dr. Kathleen Blackburn. Mr. Valdemars Blankenburgs, a member of the forest staff at Kielder, has collected specimens of bog timber preserved in the peat until unearthed by recent drainage or ploughing, and these represent birch, pine and oak. It is not easy to say, from such scanty remains, how high the forests spread up the hills, nor how tall their trees grew. But we may picture a forest cover up to elevations of 1,300 feet or so, vigorous where the natural drainage was good, and shorter or more scrubby on the ill-drained portions.

The disappearance of this forest cover was a slow process, taking many centuries to run its course, and even today patches of oak, alder, or birch scrub, together with occasional hazels, willows, ash trees, wych elms, bird cherries, hollies or rowans, may be found on the steeper slopes of the cleuchs where the ground is least accessible to sheep. Probably the highest and most isolated of these patches is in William's Cleugh, 6 miles up the Kielder and Scalp Burns above Kielder Castle. Here there is a thin band of scrub over a mile long, consisting of birch, rowan, and willow. Self-sown Scots pine trees are also found, though these may have arisen from chance seeds, wind-borne from distant plantations. This little wood lies between 1,000 and 1,250 feet in elevation.

Undoubtedly the main cause of the forest's decline has been grazing by domestic animals, in the past by cattle, ponies, and goats, but latterly almost solely by sheep. We can only guess at what period it went, but there are references in tales of the Border raiders, from the period between A.D. 1300 and 1600, to woods where the dales are now treeless. The Scots pine declined early on, but the broadleaved trees, which can withstand far more grazing, persisted longer. Perhaps it was the peaceable conditions that followed the Union of the Crowns in 1603 that first made possible the large scale open-range grazing by sheep which finished off the Border forests. Before that, when every man feared that his livestock might be reived overnight by his neighbours from over the Border, the flocks and herds could hardly be allowed to range at will. Even so, the woods vanished only gradually, for the old trees stand for centuries, although the busy sheep, by destroying every seedling or tender shoot below them, made regeneration of the woods by natural means impossible.

4

There is little evidence of widespread felling on any scale for industrial use, but from time to time cutting was no doubt done to meet emergencies such as arose during the Wars of the Roses or the Cromwellian Wars, while there are records of the Scots taking away timber during their raids. Nor is there much reason to believe that fire destroyed the original forest cover, for broadleaved woodland does not readily take fire. But after it had declined it is probable that the custom of muirburning, that is the burning away of dry herbage in spring to secure a temporary improvement of the pasture, helped to destroy any struggling saplings that had escaped the busy teeth of the sheep. For a time the sheep runs prospered, aided by the store of fertility released from the declining forest. Far from the nearest village, one can still find occasional steadings, often today in ruins, which formed their centres. For example, near the head of the Scalp Burn, 7 miles above Kielder Castle, there is a well-marked site of a croft or shieling, with a single rowan tree.

Gradually however much of the pasturage declined, through the steady accumulation of surface peat, and the ousting of the better herbage grasses by mosses, rushes, purple moor grass, deer grass, and heather, until the point was reached when many sheep farms ceased to be profitable. This setback was largely a reflection of the general decline in hill farming which affected the whole country from 1870 on. Merino wool began to be imported in increasing quantities, and there was a gradual fall in wool prices. Overseas imports, assisted by developments in cold storage, became an important influence in meat markets, and the prices of beef, wool and lamb likewise fell. As the years went on the hay intakes on the hill farms deteriorated, bracken increased with fewer cattle on the hills, drainage became poorer, and diseases took a heavier toll among breeding ewes and lambs.

It was against this background of a pastoral and economic decline that the Commission began its work; large areas of land could be obtained cheaply since their agricultural use no longer provided a living for the farmers. Forestry, albeit of a new character based on introduced coniferous trees, might be given a fresh chance on these treeless hills, to see whether timber production would now be a successful use for them. At the same time the better sheep land, and the more fertile land suitable for farming along the dale floors, could be reserved for its traditional uses.

ANTIQUITIES

Let us next see what the archaeologists can tell us regarding past settlements in early times. The Roman Wall, so well described by Professor Richmond in another chapter, lay to the south, and although there was a Roman station called Bremenium, where

5

three roads met close to Rochester in Redesdale, another at Bonchester Bridge near Hawick, and yet another called Banna at Bewcastle, the traces of Roman occupation of these hills are slight. Roman roads and occasional rectangular camps have been identified, but there is little else.

The non-Roman relics of this early period consist mainly of round fortified camps, tumuli, ditches which may have served either as boundaries or defensive works, and trackways. Considering the great area involved, they are very sparse, suggesting that this region was never densely settled. Round camps are found at Highlee Hill, near the Hyndlee portion of Wauchope Forest; near the North Tyne River at Smales in Kielder Forest; at Gibbies Knowe on the Kielder Burn; near Kielder Castle and at Highfield northwest of Greenhaugh; also in Redesdale near Elishaw, and around Otterburn. On the summit of Caerba Hill, which rises two miles south of Newcastleton and is topped by a new fire look-out tower, are the clear remains of an enclosed hut group, with stone ruins disposed in circles.

There are tumuli at Hair Cairn and Windburgh Hill in Wauchope Forest; at the head of the Currick Syke in Kershope Forest; a long cairn and a round cairn at Bell Shiel Law on the north of Redesdale; and a supposed cromlech called The Three Kings on Todlaw south of the Rede. Various hill-top mounds may have served a like purpose, but it is hard to identify tumuli today with any certainty, for the shepherds have topped many likely sites with 'ruckles of stones' to serve as landmarks when herding flocks, or as guides when the mists come down over the fells. These stone cairns are known as *curricks;* many are quite substantial and may well mask prehistoric structures. Other modern 'monuments' are the small round sheep folds dotted over the fells, and the angular walls marking the outline of old shelter woods—isolated blocks in the lee of which sheep could remain safe during blizzards. Miles of dry-stane dykes likewise stand, even where they serve only as relics of a vanished pattern of land use.

The largest prehistoric earthwork in the neighbourhood is the Catrail, or Picts Ditch, which runs from east to west near Shankendshiels, not far from the western edge of Wauchope Forest. The Wheel Causey, a pre-Roman road, can be traced right across the Hyndlee area of Wauchope Forest, running from north to south. There is an ancient standing stone on Windy Edge, in the Tinnisburn portion of Newcastleton Forest, on the western side of Liddesdale; and another one at Dinmont Lair, in Kershope Forest.

When we come to the medieval period, ample relics remain of the famous peel towers or larger castles that formed the Borderers'

6

strongholds. Liddesdale is particularly rich in them—perhaps evidence of the unruly character of its inhabitants. The most famous and best preserved of these is Hermitage Castle, now a vast and eerie ruin, which was the stronghold of the de Soulis family, and later of the Douglases. Here, in 1566, Mary Queen of Scots visited her wounded lover, Bothwell. Also in the neighbourhood of Newcastleton and Kershope Forests are the ruins of Liddel Castle, Redheugh Tower, Hartsgarth Tower, Gorrenberry Tower, Larriston Tower, Breaken Tower, Park Tower, Clintwood Castle and Greena Tower. At Bewcastle there stands the impressive ruin of the castle of the Wardens of the West March, built on the site of the old Roman Fort. Stonegarthside Hall, near Kershopefoot, is a good example of an old Border country house still inhabited.

Wauchope Forest includes the site of Wauchope Tower, with two small square forts, possibly peels, nearby; the old Wauchope House, once the home of a branch of the Scott family, has been demolished.

On the Northumberland side of the Border, the peels are not so readily identified, probably because many have continued in occupation, with gradual changes, until the present day. Mr. Valdemars Blankenburgs has studied this aspect of Border architecture, and has secured photographs which show how many of the outlying farmsteads were maintained in a defensible state until quite recent times. Often a building, now no longer a dwelling but used as a barn, has an awkward entrance which any raider would find it hard to force. Of the more famous peels we may mention Kirshope Castle, which is not in Kershope Forest but near Kielder; and Dally Castle, now in ruins, beside the Chirdon Burn near Tarset, which was once held by the Lindsays as a Scottish outpost in England. In Redesdale the highest peels up the dale are probably those at High Rochester, on the old Roman encampment of Bremenium; one is still occupied. Another peel stands east of Elishaw.

Nowadays this region is singularly poor in churches—evidence again of its thinly peopled character. Its modern parishes, on either side of the Border, are exceptionally large; but in the old days of subsistence farming, North Tynedale at least carried a larger population, and was divided into more numerous small parishes, each with its church. A map dated 1660 shows no fewer than *twenty-four* churches in the dales of the North Tyne and its tributaries, *above* Bellingham! Ecclesiastical remains of historical interest include Souden Kirk, now in ruins, near Bonchester Bridge, where in 1388 the Earl of Douglas assembled his forces for the Otterburn raid. In Liddesdale we have the remains of the old Castleton Church, with its cross; and the ruins of the old Hermitage Chapel. Bewcastle,

7

near Kershope Forest, has in its churchyard the finest sculptured cross of the Anglo-Saxon period in all Britain; it was set up about A.D. 750, according to its runic inscription, by 'Hwaetred, Wothgar, Olwfwold after (in memory of) Alcfrith, lately king and son of Oswy'; its design, which includes the figure of Christ, has exceptional artistic merit. St. Cuthbert's church at Bellingham is noteworthy for its unique roof, the great stone slabs being carried on hexagonal stone ribs without any timber; it is said that the Scots had burnt two earlier timbered roofs.

Some ten miles to the north of Wauchope Forest, as the crow flies, but considerably further if one follows the winding course of the Jed Water, the magnificent ruins of Jedburgh Abbey stand in the heart of Jedburgh town. The lands around were once known as Jed Forest, and the extensive lands of the Abbey probably included much of the modern forest. It is known too, that the monks were among the sheep owners whose flocks caused the gradual diminution of the region's ancient tree cover.

A number of old drove roads and bridle paths, some of them following the tracks of the old reivers, may be traced over the fells. A famous crossing is that of the Bloodybush, between Kielder and Newcastleton, where the old toll road now crosses the Border. The site of the Redeswire Fray, the last of all the Border battles, fought in 1575 close to Carter Bar, is also well known. At Deadwater, right on the Border above Kielder, a spa was established about 1800 on the strength of a natural spring of sulphur water, but it flourished for only a few years. The few high roads; the railway from Carlisle through Kershopefoot and Newcastleton to Hawick; the branch line, now closed, that left it at Riccarton Junction to wind down through Kielder Forest to Bellingham and Hexham; and the big Catcleugh Reservoir, built in 1907 to supply Newcastle with drinking water, complete the tale of prominent features in the forest landscape. There are remarkably few big houses in the neighbourhood; only Kielder Castle, built in 1775 at a cost of £1,300 as a shooting box for the Duke of Northumberland, and Hesleyside, close to Bellingham, call for mention. This scarcity again provides evidence of a countryside poor in natural resources; there are parks and mansions farther down the dales, but not here in the hills.

FOUNDATION OF KIELDER CASTLE

The following passage, written by Charles Williams, Governor of Kielder Castle, in an old game book, has kindly been contributed by His Grace the Duke of Northumberland.

Fixed upon in 1771, and begun in 1772, and finished 1775.

His Grace the Duke of Northumberland being desirous of erecting a Lodge on his Estate at Keelder in North Tyndal for the accommodation of his family and friends in Moor Game shooting, requested his son Earl Percy to go thither and fix on a proper place for the purpose; accordingly in the year 1771 the Earl, accompanied by Davidson Richard Grieve, Esq., of Swarland, Captain George Farquhar of Alnwick, William Charleton, Esq., of Leehall, Charles Williams of Newcastle and Roger Hall of Catcleugh met at the latter's house, slept there, and next morning rode over the Girdlestone Fell, where all the Party (the Earl excepted) with their Servants were bog'd to the no small entertainment of his Lordship and all the followers; the diversion of shooting was pursued till Noon when we arrived at Mr. William Hedley's, Rainhill, where the Earl and Messrs. Farquhar and Williams slept, and the rest at Mr. Jeremy Hedley's; next morning all the Party went in search of a spot for the foundation of the Castle, when it was unanimously agreed to erect it on the ground above the Scar, the situation presenting so fine a view of the two streams of Tyne and Keelder with the picturesque scenery of woods, hills and dale; on this mount we eat our repast, and the fine evening urging us to pursue our sports. Mr. Williams' famous Dog Pompey having sprung a Black Cock which flew to the knowl whereon the Castle now stands (at that time quite a thicket) and in trying to find him, Mr. Williams was so charmed with the situation that he summoned the Party to the ground, who all concurred in the Earl's determination to build it there; hereupon a Servant was dispatched to Hedley's for a Bottle of Wine, every Man drawn up with shoulder'd musquet, and after Success to Keelder Castle was drank by All under a general discharge, the word of command given by Governor Williams, (an Honor confer'd in the field on him by his Lordship) and the bottle broke over the butt end of his musquet to mark the Spot for laying the foundation, and a cheerful evening concluded a joyous day. Mr. William Newton was the Architect from a design of the Duke's, and Will. Robley of Smales-mouth led the Timber from Newcastle, and all the stone, lime, sand, etc. used in the Building, which was finished A.D. 1775, and Earl Percy first slept in it A.D. 1777.

Charles Williams.

OTHER ACTIVITIES

Many attempts have been made to exploit commercially the numerous shallow seams of coal that run through the region, but with only limited success. The biggest working was a drift at Plashetts, and it was to carry its coal over into Liddesdale that the toll road past the Bloody Bush was built, about 1776, by two landed proprietors. Other workings were opened beside the 'Coal Grain' stream close to the Bloody Bush itself, beside other 'Coal Grains' on both Scottish and English sides of the Kershope Burn, and even on the very summit of Carter Fell. But today the only active coal drift is one at Plashetts. The mounds of shale around such workings are apt to be confused with ancient monuments. There seems little chance of coal ever again becoming important to local economy.

According to local tradition, a stretch of flat ground close to Kershope Bridge in Kershope Forest, where the Kershope Burn forms the actual Border, was the place appointed for the periodical meetings of the Wardens of the Marches, from either side of the Border, to settle disputes by peaceable means.

The monument marked on the maps at The Wythes, some two miles to the north-east, is comparatively modern, having been erected in 1852 as a memorial to a gamekeeper named Davidson, who was murdered by poachers out on the hill. Near Deadwater, the place names of 'Peden's Pulpit' and 'Peden's Cleugh' recall the famous preacher Peden, of Scottish Covenanting days.

ARCHAEOLOGICAL FINDS

There has been little deliberate archaeological excavation on the lands that now comprise the Border forests, but from time to time chance finds have been made by forest workers. The intensive ploughing and draining that are carried on provide frequent opportunities for such discoveries, particularly as the peaty soil both preserves objects well and yields them up readily. Yet finds have been scanty—evidence again of a sparse population in past ages. Recorded objects include the following:

At Kielder Forest:
> Bronze sword of the late Bronze Age (*c.* 1,000-450 B.C.). Now in the British Museum.

At Wark Forest:
> (1) Silver seal and chain of Henricus de Bordun. Late 13th or early 14th century, A.D., British Museum. Illustrated in the *Proceedings of the Society of Antiquaries of Newcastle*, 5. Ser. I. Plate I.
> (2) Bronze Bell, Mediaeval or later. (Forestry Commission Headquarters.)
> (3) Spindle whorl of shale. (F.C.)

At Newcastleton Forest:
> (1) Fourteen silver pennies, dating from 1247 to 1260. (B.M.)
> (2) Alexander III penny. (Scottish, 1279-1285). (F.C.)
> (3) Edward I penny. (English, 1272-1307). (F.C.)

The names bestowed by the people of a region upon their landmarks can tell us a great deal, not only about the countryside but about its early inhabitants. Here on the Border they reveal unsuspected facts concerning those few people who settled there; the name Bewcastle, for example, commemorates a Norse leader named Beuth. Remarkably, there is no apparent difference between the place names on the Scottish, and those on the English, side of the Border. This supports the view advanced by Professor Mackie in his chapter on Border History, that the Border is essentially political; whatever differences may subsist elsewhere between Scots and English, here their boundary line divides people who once spoke the same tongue, and who come of a common stock. Even today, though the keen ear will detect differences between the Scottish dialects north-west of the Border and the Northumbrian or Cumbrian dialects to the south or east, the two forms of speech are barely distinguishable when set down in print. Three hundred years of Border warfare were not enough to erase the common tongue, and the Border battles were fought between kinsmen rather than between men of different races.

The characteristic Border place-name elements are typical of the hills that extend from the Lothians south to the Pennines and the Peak District, and some of them are also found in the English Lake District. They are largely Norse in character, having some words in common with the Anglian elements of the Northumbrian coastal plain, but very few words related to the Celtic place names found farther north. So far are they removed from 'standard English', that the following glossary may prove helpful to the visitor when he comes to read his Ordnance Map:

Word	Origin	Meaning
Beck	Norse, *bakki*	Stream
Bield	Norse, *bjel*	Shelter for sheep
Binks	Norse, *benk*	Shelf or bench on hillside
Bog	Gaelic, *bogach*	Marsh
Bught	Norse, *buth* = shed; originally the herdsfolk lived at the fold	Small sheepfold, particularly for ewe milking
Burn	Norse, *brunnr*	Hill stream
Cleuch, cleugh or clough	Norse, *Kleiv*	Steep sided valley or glen; cleft or ravine
Currick	Welsh, *carreg*	Cairn of Stones
Edge	Norse, *egg*	Straight ridge of rocks
Fell	Norse, *fjell*	Hillside, particularly the upper slopes
Flothers or Flow	Norse, *flo*	Peat bog, especially one that is wet and actively growing

11

Word	Origin	Meaning
Gairs or Gears	Anglo-Saxon, *gar*	Pointed piece of land where streams meet
Glen	Gaelic, *gleann*	Valley
Grain	Norse, *grein*	A branch, hence a side stream, often applied to a watercourse
Haugh	Norse, *haugr*	Flat land beside a river
Holm	Norse, *holm*	An island or a riverside plain
Hope	Norse, *hopr*	Sheltered valley
Kaim	Norse, *kamp*	Rounded hill-top or hummock
Knowe	Norse, *knoll*	Small rounded hill
Lair	Anglo-Saxon, *leger*	Sheltered hollow
Law	Anglo-Saxon, *hlaw*	Bold hill
Linn	Anglo - Saxon, *hlynn*, torrent; and Gaelic *linn*, pool	Waterfall; chasm with falls and pools together
Moss	Norse, *mose*	Peat bog, mature and suitable for cutting
Pike	Norse, *plk*	Prominent, pointed hill
Rig	Norse, *hryggr*	Ridge of a hill; sometimes old plough ridges
Shank	Norse, *skakkr*	Long spur of hill
Shaw	Norse, *skogr*	Wood
Shiels or Shields	Norse, *skale* or *skjol*	Upland summer grazings
Sike	Norse, *sik*	Ditch, runnel, or straight watercourse
Slack	Norse, *slakki*	Hollow amid the hills
Spout	Norse, *spyta*	Waterfall
Stell	Norse, *stallr*, stall	Sheepfold
Toft	Norse, *toft*	Homestead

NAMES OF FORESTS, ETC.

Kielder, Norse *kelda*, a spring.

Wark, from the village.

Redesdale, from the dale of the River Rede.

Kershope, after the Kershope Burn; *ker*, from Norse *kjarr*, marshy alder wood, refers to flat lands at Kershopefoot; *hopr* is Norse for valley.

Newcastleton, after the town, so called when founded in 1800, to house the people from Castleton, near the Castle higher up Liddesdale. Still called Copshaw Holm, the original name of the site, by local people.

Wauchope, Norse *valgr hopr*, warm valley.

Bellingham, pronounced Bellinjam, is from Anglo-Saxon, and means 'the home of Bella's people'; Bell remains a local surname.

Deadwater. Slow stream. The land here is flat and forms the watershed between the North Tyne and the Liddel.

Otterburn. The burn or stream of the otters.

Bonchester Bridge. Latin *bonus castra*, the good camp. One of the few 'chester' place names in Scotland; it dates from the Roman occupation.

SHEEP FARMING

During what one may term the romantic period of the Border wars and their associated literature, the agricultural economy of the region was largely on a subsistence basis. Each family produced its necessities, meat, milk, butter, cheese, wool for homespun and handwoven clothing; and hides for leather, from its own flocks and herds. Although these hills are little suited for arable cultivation, oats were grown for meal, wheat for flour, and barley for home-brewed beer, on a scale sufficient to satisfy the local people.

With the passing of the old Border warfare, it became more profitable to concentrate on sheep raising, in order to export the readily saleable wool and mutton to distant markets for cash returns; other forms of husbandry then gradually declined. At first the hillsides had no boundaries, but each herdsman knew the extent of his grazings, which were demarcated by rows of cairns or curricks along the ridges. Since sheep are creatures of habit, and remain attached to their native *cut* or *hirsel*, they wander less than one might expect; but various brands or ear marks are used so that each man's stock may be identified if it strays. Gradually a network of drystane dykes was built up to separate the grazing grounds. On the Cumberland side there were extensive common grazings, particularly in the big parish called Nicholforest; but about the end of the eighteenth century these were divided among the farmers who held grazing rights, by a series of Enclosure Acts and awards, and many medium-sized farms resulted. Gradually the remoter hills were split into bigger farms, averaging around 2,000 acres of hill grazing with a few score acres of better land around the steadings; some were freehold, but the great 47,000 acre Kielder estate, owned by the Duke of Northumberland, included many tenanted farms.

In Liddesdale, where there were many cottars and crofters, the model town of Newcastleton was laid out, about 1800, to accommodate them, after their scattered holdings had been amalgamated into big sheep farms.

Besides the land selected for afforestation, some 50,000 acres of the Border forests have been set aside for retention under agriculture. This includes most of the better hill grazings, also those poorer ones that occupy land too high-lying for profitable timber growing, and also virtually all the improved land down in the dales. Where necessary, these farms have been re-shaped, or have had their land regrouped, to provide economic units. In particular, some of those in the dale bottoms are concentrating on dairy produce, for which the new forest communities provide a local market. Though some farms have been afforested, others have gained a fresh lease of life. Other farms again have been divided into smallholdings for Forest Workers. These adjustments of agricultural land have been carried out in close co-operation with the Ministry of Agriculture, Fisheries and Food in England, or with the Department of Agriculture and Fisheries in Scotland.

Where sheep farming continues, it is mainly based on the hardy Scottish black-face and Swaledale breeds, which spend the winter out on the exposed hillsides; Cheviots and North Country Cheviots are however favoured on some of the better ground. In spring, the ewes are brought down to the lower slopes for lambing. Later they return with their lambs to the high fells, but during the spring and summer they are again gathered in for dipping and shearing. Some of the young ewes are sent away to the low country of the Northumberland or Cumberland plains, or to low ground in the Tweed Valley, for their first winter, but in subsequent winters they live out on the hill. The blackfaced sheep yield a coarse type of wool which is not of high value for cloth, but is excellent for carpets and similar hard-wearing textiles; the Cheviots provide a better fleece, suitable for clothing. In addition to wool and lambs, the hill flocks are a source of breeding ewes which are usually mated to rams of other breeds, such as the Border Leicester, on lowland farms, to produce cross-bred lambs which mature rapidly for the butcher. The hill farmer's returns come partly from the sale of wether lambs and surplus ewes, partly from the wool, and partly from young cattle.

The shepherd's life is a pleasant, if lonely one in summer, but he has to be out of doors at all hours, and in all weathers, throughout the year. Winter blizzards which may engulf his flocks in deep snow-drifts and threaten them with starvation, are a particularly trying time. These men know every nook in the hills, which they range from dawn to dusk with great assurance, self reliance, and staying power. Each has the companionship of one or more sheepdogs, of the black-and-white Border collie breed, which interpret the whistled signals unfailingly, and round up the wandering sheep with uncanny accuracy.

THE NEW FOREST VILLAGES

The planned afforestation of 135,000 acres of land has led to a great increase in local employment, and to the need for more houses to accommodate the workpeople. The existing farm houses can do little to help here, for where possible the farms are kept going, and where that is impracticable it is often because they are too remote to attract people today. A glance at the map will show that, except at Newcastleton, the existing towns or villages, such as Bellingham, Wark, and Otterburn, lie some miles from the forests, so that the labour drawn therefrom must be transported quite a distance to its daily work. At first the need for labour was met by taking over what few cottages were available, as they fell vacant, for forest workers. A number of new cottages or bungalows were also built, being associated as a rule with smallholdings; in all there are ninety such Forest Workers Holdings in the Border Forests.

The end of the war in 1945 coincided with a growing demand for labour to start the essential and continuing work of thinning the plantations, and it became obvious that this could only be met by building new houses on a large scale. In the Northumbrian forests, the method chosen has been the formation of Forest Villages, while in Cumberland and Roxburghshire large groups of houses, usually near existing settlements, have sufficed. The help of Dr. Thomas Sharp, the well-known town planning consultant, was enlisted to secure appropriate designs for the Northumbrian villages, together with attractive aspects that would blend with the scenery of the now forest-clad fells.

The numbers of houses built under various schemes, are as follows:

Kielder Forest:	At Kielder Village, close to Kielder Castle . .	63
Wark Forest:	At Stonehaugh, four miles west of Wark village .	35
Redesdale Forest:	At Byrness, beside the main Jedburgh road ten miles north-west of Otterburn	47
Kershope Forest:	Two main groups, one at Kershopefoot in Liddesdale, the other at Sleetbeck, five miles east of Liddesdale along the secondary road from Langholm to Haltwhistle	44
Newcastleton Forest:	At Holmfoot, beside Newcastleton village . .	10
Wauchope Forest:	22 close to Bonchester Bridge, south of the main Hawick-Newcastle road, six miles from Hawick; 6 others in the forest	28
Total for six Forests		227

Taking the Forest Workers Holdings and the new village houses together, it will be seen that the Forestry Commission has provided some 300 modern dwellings in these six forests. The number of workers so housed is rather greater, since it is common for more than

15

one wage-earner to come from each dwelling. The number of wage-earners may therefore be estimated at 450, and their dependants at a further 900 people. Thus about 1,350 people have already been housed in modern dwellings in the Border Forests, and this number is sure to grow as the increasing demand for labour calls for extensions to the present villages.

In their lay-out, the new villages follow the current pattern of groups of houses set well clear of main roads, with broad access roads and ample playing greens for the children. The houses are substantially built and well planned internally, and are let at moderate rents to the Commission's employees. Water supplies and sanitary arrangements have been provided on modern lines, and electric power is available.

A village, however, consists of something more than a cluster of houses, and much thought has been given to the provision of the varied amenities required by a modern rural community. The solutions vary with local circumstances at each village. The lack of shops is not felt so keenly as one might expect, for the district is well served with travelling vans. But general shops, often combined with post-offices, can now be found at Kielder, Byrness, Stonehaugh and Kershopefoot. Milk, of course, comes from local farms. Communications with the outer world present a problem, though some forest workers run cars. But at Newcastleton and Kershopefoot, railways are at hand, while Byrness, Bonchester Bridge and Kielder have daily bus services. Stonehaugh and Sleetbeck, however, have to rely on buses which run only on certain days of the week.

The need for social life makes itself felt early, in the demand for a village hall; sites for such halls have been reserved at all the villages, and temporary buildings have already been put up. At Kielder rooms in the Castle have been converted into a social club. Land has also been set aside for playing fields. These amenities are organised by local clubs or committees, who rent the land or building from the Forestry Commission.

The provision of schools is of course the concern of the county educational authorities, but here again the Commission helps by providing suitable sites; good modern schools have recently been built at Byrness and Kielder. Other sites have been earmarked for churches; while another possible future development is the building of hotels to cater for both the local people and for visitors. Co-operation is maintained with the various departments of the local authorities who provide such services as public health and travelling libraries.

One or two of the villages still have a rather incomplete air, as though they have not yet had time to grow accustomed to their

Byrness Village in Redesdale Forest, looking towards the Border

Kielder Castle

Felling a Spruce in Manse Wood, Kielder

Darts in the Kielder Club

At Play in Kielder Village

Washing Day

The Roman Wall

Clintburn Farm, Chirdon, a Typical Hill Farm Built in a Strategic Situation

surroundings. But as their gardens are developed, and their ornamental trees grow taller and provide shade and shelter, and as the various auxiliary buildings and sportsfields are added to the rows of bold, white-walled houses, they will fit more serenely into the landscape.

We have seen that few people were available in these dales to work the new woods, and in practice most of the villagers have come to the Border forests from other districts. Though work at fair wages is assured, and good housing has been provided, not every family of newcomers has been prepared to accept the dual change of job and surroundings. Some have moved on after but a short stay, but gradually there are being assembled groups of people who intend to settle for good amid the healthy surroundings of the young hillside forests, and to play their part in building up living communities that they can regard as home. Many of these new Borderers come from the industrial towns of Tyneside, Cumberland or Central Scotland, to which their forefathers migrated only a generation or two ago; and some have always maintained links with their native countryside.

A helmet of the legion, this,
  That long and deep hath lain,
Come back to taste the living kiss
  Of sun and wind again.
Ah! touch it with a reverent hand,
  For in its burnished dome
Lies here within this distant land
  The glory that was Rome!

On a Roman Helmet found at Newstead—W. H. Ogilvie

THE BORDER REGION IN ROMAN TIMES

BY PROFESSOR I. A. RICHMOND

The Roman domination of Northern Britain lasted from A.D. 71 until at least A.D. 400; and for upwards of two centuries during that epoch the Border between England and Scotland, as our region was later to be known, formed the border of the Roman province. But more than a century of experiment, varied and prolonged, was to be undertaken before this solution, so intimately in harmony with the physical characteristics of the region, came to be reached.

It was at first an experiment made in optimism. The governor Iulius Agricola, who undertook the enlargement of Roman power from the Vale of York to the Highland gates, expected to conquer the whole island. Only the uninviting desolation and peculiar natural configuration of the Highlands prevented him from doing so. But his methods in the hinterland of his conquests left an indelible mark upon the Border landscape. The main north road from York to the Forth and beyond, later called Dere Street by Saxon and Norman, threaded its way across County Durham from Tees to

Tyne, and then struck boldly for the Cheviot Hills. Its course is only partly followed by modern roads, from Corbridge to Elishaw, a junction between Otterburn and Rochester on the modern highway from Newcastle to Carter Bar; but it is a brilliant piece of engineering, in which reconnaissance has seized, with unerring eye, the watershed course from Tyne to Kale Water. From Featherwood to the Kale Water it is as the Romans left it, ruined now by age-long weathering or neglect, but still exhibiting the broad mound which formed its skeleton, the quarry-pits whence its metalling was hewn, and the bold determined zig-zags by which it climbed the steepest slopes. Not a motorists' choice of gradient: the hills are often short and sharp, suited to horses rather than horse-power. The camber, too, is steeper than tar-macadam requires. The result is still a moving relic of human achievement and endeavour, worthy to rank with the railway which is its modern peer.

This was not the only Border road laid down by Rome. North of Corbridge Dere Street threw off a branch, later called by awe-struck country folk the Devil's Causeway, which ran north-east-wards across Northumberland to Berwick-on-Tweed; and a cross-road through Holystone and Lorbottle (near Whittingham) linked this again with Dere Street where the two had separated widely. This was typical of Agricolan policy, to surround the native communities with garrisons, cordoning them off for military and fiscal control. In this net the garrisons and their forts formed the knots, the roads the cords which held all together.

Forts of the period are known at Corbridge on the Tyne, and at High Rochester, just north of the modern village of Rochester in Redesdale, both on Dere Street; also at Learchild, near Whittingham, on the Devil's Causeway; and although the two former lie buried deep below *later* Roman remains, their size defines their garrison. At Corbridge lay in garrison the largest cavalry regiment in the province, one thousand strong, ready to strike northward or north-eastward or westward across the Tyne-Solway isthmus. High Rochester held a part-mounted infantry regiment, 500 strong. At Learchild, what is known of the work suggests a cavalry regiment, five hundred strong. These units could dragoon the newly-con-quered district into order, inculcating obedience to the tax-gatherer and the conscription-officer, and supervising the markets which, outside the forts or at native fair-grounds, introduced the advantages of widening commerce and a guaranteed peace.

Apart from these permanent garrisons soldiers were little in evidence off the main lines of communications. But Dere Street at Sills Burn or at Featherwood, both north of High Rochester, or at Chew Green further north and right on the modern Border, exhibits some notable examples of the bivouac camps nightly erected by troops on the march or prepared for a longer stay by squads engaged upon road-construction or repair. Chew Green boasts in addition a tiny convoy-post at a particularly difficult point on the Coquet defiles.

Agricola's northward movement had begun in A.D. 79, and was sealed in A.D. 84 by a victory at the Highland gates, so great that it was thought feasible to reduce the military garrison. Consolidation then followed about A.D. 90 and virtually no change was made in the arrangement of the occupied area, except that forts were strengthened and communications manifestly improved. The first major change came not long after A.D. 103, when all the territory north of the Cheviots was abandoned, either in response to enemy pressure or to economise still further in man-power. The firmest line now held was the cross-route from Corbridge to Carlisle. But there is some reason for thinking that Northumberland was not wholly abandoned and that Blakehope fort at Elishaw Bridge may be a product of the new situation, in the form of an outpost guarding the Rede bridgehead. It is, however, clear that a fixed northern frontier was becoming imperative and further troubles, at the opening of Hadrian's reign in A.D. 117, underlined the need. The answer to the problem was Hadrian's Wall.

No ancient monument in Britain is more romantic or evocative than Hadrian's Wall, as succeeding generations discover afresh for themselves. Its 72-mile course, from Wallsend on the Tyne to Bowness-on-Solway, is everywhere of interest, but in the wilder lands between the North Tyne and Irthing rivers it holds imagination enthralled. It was first planned as a patrolled barrier, with forts at some distance behind it. In this way sentinels worked on the Wall itself from regularly-spaced turrets and milecastles, the latter with gates to north and south; while the fort-garrisons could move freely through the Wall to intercept and corral raiders. But almost at once this initial scheme was tightened up. The forts were transferred to the line of the Wall itself, and the rear of the whole work was cut off by a great boundary-ditch, known as the Vallum, from its prominent upcast mounds. The Vallum converted the new frontier into a continuous zone impregnably defended on the north and completely screened from thieves and outlaws on the South. Even then more forts were added, until the ten first supplied on the Wall itself became fifteen.

Nor was this all. In the West, where the outlook from the Wall is poor, more outpost forts were part of the scheme from the first. Watch-towers and mile fortlets also continued down the Cumberland coast, and on their line, as on the Wall, forts were quickly

20

added. The date of the work is generally attested by literature and given in more detail by inscriptions. The wall, its milecastles and turrets, were built under the governor Platorius Nepos, whose term of office began in July A.D. 122, and continued until about A.D. 126. This governor was also responsible for the transference of forts on to the line of the wall itself. The further additions of forts, however, belong to a little later, and it is clear that the work continued until the early thirties when Carrawburgh (west of Chollerford) and Carvoran (east of Greenhead) were in course of erection. A little more than a decade was thus needed for the whole operation, but each winter season must have brought the work to a stop and the working time taken is accordingly reduced.

The intention of the builders appears to have been from the first a double one. The Wall served as an impenetrable barrier against infiltration, in terrain where clandestine movement in small numbers was very difficult to control, as the stories of countless Border forays in a later age testify. But, by virtue of its regular system of gateways, the Wall could also be used as a base for sallies intended to round up attackers against the barrier itself, and it provided the corral necessary to such tactics in country otherwise devoid of continuous natural obstacles. There can be little doubt that by its very nature the Wall performed these tasks successfully. Yet there is ample evidence, in the many modifications of the original scheme, that it provoked a sharper hostile reaction than its designers had anticipated, and that even in the rear of the work there was more petty thieving than had been foreseen. Only so is it possible to explain the transference of forts, the creation of the Vallum, and the addition of still further forts when the main lines of approach had already been blocked. The thieving is probably less due to downright hostility than to the incorrigibility of mankind. But the mounting precautions against attack denote at the least a growing hostility north of the Wall and indicate that, however successful the new measures may have proved, the original designers had underestimated the effect of their great cordon.

The nuisance value of such raiding from the north had only to reach a certain point to make a radical cure seem the better policy; and the position was certainly aggravated by the fact that the homes of most of the raiders lay well beyond the reach of ordinary patrolling from the Wall, in fact beyond the Cheviot hills and Liddesdale. The Northumbrian plain appears to have been quieter and more peaceable, to judge from the absence of additional forts, except at Wallsend, and from the fact that the senior regiment on the Wall, the *Ala Petriana*, one thousand strong, lay in the west, at Stanwix just outside Carlisle.

21

The radical measures were not very long in coming. As soon as Hadrian died, new action was taken. In A.D. 139 preparations were in full swing for the reoccupation of Scotland under the governor Q. Lollius Urbicus. This involved a new fort at Corbridge, where the Trajanic fort had been kept in commission though unoccupied in force. A new fort on a new site was built at Risingham (Habitanicum) at the crossing of the Rede below West Woodburn, while the old site at High Rochester, at the foot of the Sills Burn valley, was unoccupied. Each fort held a part-mounted infantry regiment, 500 strong. Chew Green received a new fortlet or convoy post with two large wagon-parks attached; and the camp of the labour-force which built them still looms large on the ground or on an air-photograph. It was not now convoys alone that concerned the little garrison. On Brownhart Law, the local summit of the frontier hills, a long-distance signal-station was linked with Rubers Law in Teviotdale and so with the North Eildon at Newstead on the Tweed. In this way the entire Border area could be surveyed and alerted with great rapidity, and it need hardly be supposed that these three known signal-posts were the beginning or end of the scheme.

It is, however, surely significant for relations with the native populace that the posts at Rubers Law and the North Eildon occupied the sites of native hill-forts (*oppida*) now laid desolate. And in this connexion it must be recalled that heavy transportations of native *Brittones*, as the inhabitants of north Britain were called, were made at this time to Germany, though it is nowhere indicated from precisely which northern district they came.

Another significant point is that, while Dere Street from Tyne to Forth is relatively lightly garrisoned, if with a heavy concentration at Newstead on the Tweed, the corresponding road on the west is thickly sown with small posts for patrols, as if the west and centre of southern Scotland were sharply segregated from one another. This would be comprehensible enough if both areas had been sources of trouble, perhaps in one of those combinations of tribes as dangerous as they were rare. In this matter the truth cannot now be discerned, but its archaeological framework begins to stand out. The treatment of the Northumberland coastal plain at this time is not yet clear. It lay within the newly-acquired territory and is inherently likely to have received a garrison. But the details of distribution and composition are as yet unknown.

The new wall, known as Antonine's Wall, between Forth and Clyde received, it is clear, many of the regiments formerly in garrison on Hadrian's Wall. But this does not mean that the forts of Hadrian's Wall remained empty. New garrisons took their place, composed of detachments of legionaries. The patrolling system on

Hadrian's Wall was on the other hand for the time being abandoned. The doors were removed from the milecastle gateways, leaving them as unhindered thoroughfares; the milecastle and turret garrisons disappeared. Above all, the rearward boundary or Vallum was now systematically breached or slighted, by breaches through the mounds and causeways across the ditches, at every 45 yards. The barrier was then abolished though its line was still garrisoned, and the act marks the extension of the province northwards to the narrower isthmus. This state of affairs, however, was to last barely a generation. It seems that the new forward movement had been achieved only by stripping the Pennine area of troops. And, while the Vale of York, or other favourable lands here and there, might be the scene of growing Romanisation, much of the Pennine region and the tribe of the Brigantes to which it belonged still comprised primitive and semi-nomadic folk whose wealth lay in flocks and herds and whose lives were irritated rather than improved by Roman rule and its burdens. Conscription and taxation, even though accompanied by peace, were too little compensated by amelioration of the daily lot.

By A.D. 155–158 the district had broken into violent revolt and unrest, and a re-occupation of the Pennine area followed a war for which substantial reinforcements had been drafted direct to the Tyne from overseas. A concentration of troops on the lower isthmus, between the Tyne and the Solway, had plainly been required in order to keep the trouble from spreading, and the value of interposing a force or a barrier at this point was promptly underlined by the re-occupation of Hadrian's Wall as a patrolled work. The milecastles and turrets came into use once again. What happened further north is not in detail demonstrable. But it is certain that the Antonine Wall was in due course re-occupied, and in itself likely that this took place soon. From now onwards the northern occupation lasted until the end of the century, although in A.D. 181 Antonine's Wall was breached by a violent and destructive northern raid. This event, however, which evoked a sharp Roman punitive campaign, was not reflected in the land between the Walls, which appears to exhibit only the destruction associated with the troubles of A.D. 155–158.

It was thus a period of pragmatic experiment and shaping policy in the light of experience that came to an end at the close of the second century. Britain was then involved in a disastrous political adventure when its governor Clodius Albinus stripped the province of troops to support his claim to the Roman principate and was defeated with heavy casualties in A.D. 197. The northern tribes broke into the military area and brought almost total destruction as far south as York, and this demanded not only a total rebuilding of the northern defences but a complete re-assessment of policy.

The restoration was carried out gradually, and the rebuilding of the Wall was completed between A.D. 205–208. To these years belongs also a remarkable inscription from the south gate at Risingham, now in Newcastle upon Tyne. It commemorates the rebuilding of the gate and wall of the fort, and actual remains show that these were constructed in most lavish style, with the magnificent local sandstone, which was used in modern times for the Usher Hall in Edinburgh. The fort held a part-mounted garrison twice as large as before, and the same size of regiment was quartered at High Rochester. The doubling of the strength implies a new policy, which must be taken in connexion with what was now happening upon Hadrian's Wall. Here the use of the milecastles as the basis for local sallies and rounding-up operations is brought to an end, as is demonstrated by the reduction of their gates to small posterns, useful only for parties engaged in maintaining the travelling work. Many turrets were also disused, so that the regularity of patrolling was broken. Contrariwise, the forts show signs of increased garrisons, in consonance with the provisions in the forward area just described. The picture is one of larger and more mobile garrisons operating over a wider field on the Roman part, while the enemy may be taken to be raiding in rather larger war bands. This may well be a reflection of the conditions which the defenceless province had recently been meeting, when bolder piratical expeditions from the North must have been frequent.

These events are to be dated to A.D. 208 at latest and they were followed by two years of punitive campaigning in Scotland. Five years later another development of the picture is discernible. An inscription of A.D. 213 indicates that Risingham was the seat of command not only for a part-mounted infantry regiment one thousand strong but for two units of irregulars, the *Raeti Gaesati* and the *Exploratores*. Evidence of the same date for High Rochester (Bremenium) is lacking; but by A.D. 242 *Exploratores Bremenienses* are associated with this site also. There is, however, no room at either fort for the irregulars and these must have been out-stationed. There are suggestive records of both the *Raeti Gaesati* from Risingham and the *Vardulli* from High Rochester at Jedburgh, and an outpost so far ahead would anticipate certain states of the mediaeval Border between England and Scotland. But the *Exploratores*, to judge from analogies, will have comprised communities settled in the area of the forts, whose men served on a territorial basis. It is the kind of development which took place widely in northern Britain in the third century, when many irregular units appear as additions

The Gatehouse, Tarset, an Old Fortified Farmstead

Hermitage Castle in Liddesdale

Black-faced Sheep amid the Snows at Ravenshill, Kielder

Norway Spruce in Snow, Whickhope, Kielder

to a regular garrison. But it is of great interest to find it beyond the Wall. The arrangement implies not merely a social change but a strategical innovation, by which the engineered barrier of the Wall, with its advantages of short length and good lateral communications, was retained; while at the same time the occupied zone beyond the Wall had now gone forward to the natural boundary on the southern edge of the Tweed basin, which was for centuries the march between England and Scotland.

The realities of frontier life and frontier warfare are underlined a little later at High Rochester by two inscriptions of A.D. 219–20 and A.D. 225–235 respectively. Each commemorates the re-building of a *ballistarium* or artillery platform. Excavation in 1935 demonstrated what these structures were like, revealing a massive platform 32 feet from back to front. They also produced the missiles, stone balls weighing about one hundredweight. The terrain at both High Rochester and Risingham is admirably adapted to this kind of defence and demands an effective range of some 250 yards, to cover the main lines of approach. This is a distinct development of weight and range as compared with the first century A.D., and is also a development in another respect, that, whereas in earlier days legionaries alone handled such weapons, they are now issued to auxiliary troops.

The third century is thus the most striking period in the history of the Roman occupation of the Forest area north of the Wall; to which age the fine masonry of the wall at Risingham belongs. But no less splendid is the west wall and west gate of High Rochester (*Bremenium*), which belongs, as excavation has proved, to the restoration of Constantius I, soon after A.D. 297. This restoration followed the nine-year defection of Britain under the usurpers Carausius (287–293) and Allectus (293–296), and the northern invasion which ensued upon the defeat of the latter. The new arrangements, so far as the forts were concerned, closely resembled the old, but nothing is known of irregulars or their settlements.

In A.D. 343 came a retrenchment. A crisis, of which the true nature eludes us, brought Constans across the Channel in midwinter; and one of the results was the evacuation of High Rochester and the reconstruction of both Risingham and the corresponding outpost fort of Bewcastle in the west. This phase in devolution reads like failure. But it must be taken with the picture of Roman relations with the *Votadini*, the tribe occupying Northumberland and Lothian. At their central hillfort of Traprain Law, Roman commerce had been steadily growing from the later third century onwards, and continued steady until the opening of the fifth century. When, therefore, Roman troops are wholly withdrawn from the zone

25

beyond the wall, after the great attack of Picts, Saxons and Irish in A.D. 367–9, and when the Wall itself is garrisoned with *limitanei* or farmer-soldiers, this does not imply worsening relations with the inhabitants beyond. On the contrary, it means that the problem had changed and that in an age of more mobile overseas raiders the static frontier was no longer of prime importance. The northern frontier could be left to the farmer-soldier and to the goodwill of the buffer-states beyond it, while the defence of the province became a problem for mobile units widely spaced throughout its length and breadth.

A detailed account of the Roman antiquities of Redesdale and the Northumberland side of the Border is given in the *Northumberland County History*, vol. XV.

Of Liddisdale the common theifis
Sa pertlie steilis now and reifis
    That nane may keep
    Hose, nolt,[1] nor sheep
    Nor yit dar sleep
For their mischieifis

—Sir Richard Maitland

BORDER HISTORY

BY PROFESSOR J. D. MACKIE

The Border counties are generally understood to be Northumberland, Cumberland, and Westmorland, and perhaps one might add the Palatinate of Durham, in England; and in Scotland, the shires of Berwick, Roxburgh and Dumfries with the addition, possibly, of Selkirk behind Roxburgh and Kirkcudbright to the west of Dumfries and along the Solway. Of these counties, however, only Northumberland and Cumberland in England, and Berwick, Roxburgh and Dumfries in Scotland impinge on the actual Border line.

That line runs from Berwick to Solway, a distance of only seventy miles as the crow flies; but the length of the actual frontier is about a hundred and twenty miles. The general direction from Berwick is markedly south-west, and this is a point worth noting because one is apt to assume that the Border runs due east and west. It is not so. Two of the three 'Marches' into which the English Border was divided after 1381 confronted the County of Northumberland.

The nature of the line demands attention. From Berwick it follows the line of the Tweed to Carham near Coldstream. Thence it runs south and even a little to the east of south to the 'Hanging Stone' near the peak of Cheviot; from there turning south-west again, it follows roughly the crest of the hills past Carter Fell and

[1]hose=horses; nolt=cattle.

27

Peel Fell. Thereafter it goes down the Kershope Burn to its confluence with the Liddel Water, and down the Liddel till it reaches the Esk. It does not, however, follow the Esk to the sea; on the contrary it soon leaves that stream, runs east for some miles and then drops due south along the river Sark till it debouches into the head of the Solway near Gretna.

This frontier, obviously, though in a general way it conforms to the topography of the area, is not very clearly delimited by physical features.

As the history of Franco-German relations shows clearly, a river is not a good natural boundary, since the cultures which develop on each side of its bed are apt to be very similar. Yet a river is at least a conspicuous boundary, and in so far as it followed the Tweed, the line of the Border is clear enough. In the mass of the Cheviots, however, its course is less well marked; one Border hill is very like another. There are approaches to the line both from the South up the streams of Coquet, Rede and Tyne, and from the north up the tributaries which flow into the Tweed, while through the hills themselves are passages which, though rough, were convenient for light 'rank-riders'. Some of these passages, like that up Bowmont Water over Cocklaw and into Coquetdale, were well-known routes for thieves, and 'historical evidence shows that between the Cheviot and Kershopehead there were no fewer than thirteen passages'. [Tough. *The Last Years of a Frontier*, 1928 p.29]. An alternative estimate gives twenty-three passages into Redesdale alone, and seven into Tynedale.

Further west things were hardly less difficult. The streams of Kershope and Liddel are not considerable and the Esk, which is larger, did not serve as a frontier save for a very brief distance. As might be expected the English were inclined to say that the boundary was not the Liddel, but the Tarras Water which flows into the Esk further north, and that it was continued beyond the Esk by the Irvine Burn, which comes in from the western bank. The Scots on the other hand tended to assert that their boundary was not the Sark, which runs parallel to the Esk, but the Esk itself. Neither side made good its claim, and for centuries the whole area was known as the Debateable Lands.

An official limit indeed, was arranged in September 1552 in accordance with the Treaty of Norham (1551), and according to this the Scots obtained all that lay to the north of a line which left the Esk just south of its confluence with the Liddel and ran a very little north of due west to a point just below 'Sandy Armstrong's Tower' on the Sark.

This artificial line was marked only by a furrow with a dressed stone at each end, and needless to say, the whole area, inhabited largely by Grahams in the south and Armstrongs in the north, gave shelter to broken men on each side of the Border, and became a thorn in the flesh to both governments. Even in the East March, which was far more open, there were a few small parcels of land which remained in dispute; but these were small and some of them were pastured 'indifferently' by English and Scots.

That the Border is somewhat 'untidy' is due to the fact that it came into being for political rather than geographical reasons; it was the empiric result of the ebb and flow of actual power.

The island of Britain is not large but from very early times it housed two distinct monarchies. The germ of the English realm was the kingdom of Wessex in the south, while the Scottish realm sprang from the Scoto-Pictish kingdom in the north. The Saxon power moved north, the Scoto-Pictish power moved south, and each gradually absorbed part of the country which lay between. Over this 'No Man's Land' the stronger power naturally penetrated the more deeply and took the firmer grip. Its progress, however, was interrupted by the Scandinavian incursions; these not only barred the English advance but brought about sporadic alliances between the English and the Scottish kings, and cut off the Anglian population of Lothian and Northumbria from their kinsmen in the south. By the time of the Norman Conquest Scotland had advanced her frontier to the Tweed and south of the Solway and possessed, partly by virtue of Malcolm III's marriage to English Margaret, claims over Northumbria and Cumbria; these claims were strengthened when (about 1114) Malcolm's son David I married Matilda the heiress of Waltheof. On the other hand the strong Norman and Angevin kings asserted a claim of suzerainty over Scotland. This they made good in its entirety only between 1174 and 1189; but they continued to assume an attitude of Superiority, and by granting to the Kings of Scots certain lands, some of them close to the Border (at one time, Tynedale), ensured that the Scots kings must do them homage. In these circumstances the position of the actual Border remained obscure.

Even after 1189 when the Treaty of Canterbury, in recognising the independence of Scotland, provided that the Marches between the realms should lie as they had lain before 1174, it was still not clear where those Marches were; and it was only after 1237 when Alexander II resigned his claim on English land in exchange for two hundred librates (pounds' worth) in Northumberland and Cumberland that exact definition became desirable.

Definition was required with regard to both territory and to political authority, but at first it was attained with relative ease since the populations on either side of the Border were akin in blood and in general development. Attempts to fix boundaries and to settle differences were made by appointing commissions of equal numbers of knights from England and Scotland; an effort had been made to fix one part of the line by this means in 1222. In 1243 a jury of twelve knights, six from each side, perambulated part of the Marches, without reaching agreement; and in 1249 a jury of twelve from each side produced some *leges et consuetudines marchiarum inter Scotiam et Angliam* as they are called in the Acts of the Parliaments of Scotland [I,41 3], where they are found not only in Latin but in a Scots version which cannot be contemporary. The arrangements then made were conditioned by the fact that, in those days, trial by battle was considered as the normal way in which landed men should settle disputes, and some of the regulations were concerned with the proper conduct of judicial combat. Yet here may be seen an early stage of what was afterwards known as the 'Law of the Marches'.

The development of this Law, however, was rudely interupted. The ambition of Edward I broke the peaceful relations between Scotland and England. When the English monarchs occupied great tracts of Scotland, the name 'Borders' had no significance. It is true that when Scottish independence was formally recognised in 1328 one of the stipulations of the Treaty of Edinburgh/Northampton was that the 'Laws of the Marches' should be well kept; but the bellicose Edward III soon renewed his claim of suzerainty and it was not until after the release of David II from captivity in 1357 that Scotland and England faced one another again in the old fashion. In 1367 a definite treaty was made whereby a number of representatives from each side were appointed to control the Borders. It is significant that among their representatives are found the bearers of the great Border names, Percies, Cliffords, Douglases and Homes; for the blunt truth is that in feudal times, it was the magnates rather than the crown who defended the frontier. Even when the central government was developing fast in the south of England, the north remained in the hands of the holders of the great 'liberties' within whose area the royal writ did not run, and in Scotland the power of the crown developed even more slowly.

The struggles between England and Scotland upon the Borders are often, and not without justice, regarded as a rivalry between Percy and Douglas, and on each side of the frontier the great protagonist was supported by loyal followers of famous names. For example, Nevilles, Cliffords, Scropes and Dacres, on the one side; Kerrs, Scotts, Johnstones and Maxwells on the other, were among the men who did the business.

Yet on neither side of the line did the central government stand aloof. Each monarch tried to regularise the position of the champions of his country by establishing a formal system into which the energies of their subjects could be absorbed. In the Treaty of 1367, reference is made to an East and West March, and after 1381 the English frontier was divided into three. Of these the East March with its great fortress at Berwick was the most important, and at some periods seems to have exercised superiority over the Middle March whose stronghold was Harbottle. The West March, based on Carlisle, was smaller and weaker than that of the East. Each of the Marches had its own Warden.

Even after the system was established its working was hindered by the mutual jealousies of Wardens, and by the fact that the crown could not always trust its own officers. Sometimes, as in the case of Richard II in 1385, Henry IV in 1400 and Richard of York in 1482, a Royal Prince himself came north; sometimes as when Surrey came in 1522 a trusted soldier was sent up from the south; sometimes as under Richard III and later under Henry VIII a Council representing the central government was set up at York; but whatever happened, the old families long retained their authority.

It was only after the suppression of the Rising of the North in 1569 that the royal power really took control and even though some of the Wardens were the Queen's kinsmen (Hunsdon for example, and his sons) others were representatives of the old houses. A Carey and Willoughby might come to the East March; but a Eure (until 1598) and a Scrope (until 1603) remained in the Middle March and in the West March.

In Scotland the development was the same; but it proceeded more slowly. After the return of James I from his English captivity, the East and West Marches took on a more definite appearance and, in 1451, a Middle March appeared though it seems to have been dependant upon the West March. Thereafter there were sometimes two Wardens and sometimes three, and the offices were held generally by magnates who had power in their own names. Even more than in England, however, the Crown was fain to maintain its authority by sending special commissioners *ad hoc*, and in the sixteenth century it was obviously the case that the best guarantee of good justice on the Border was a personal visit by the King. James IV in 1504 and 1510, James V in 1529 and 1530, came down with power, and the phrase 'Jeddart Justice' attests the action of the one as the fate of 'Johnnie Armstrong' does that of the other. As late as 1597 James VI of Scotland (James I of England) came to Dumfries to enforce the delivery of pledges, and to hang thieves; and he came again in 1600 and 1602.

None the less, though the organisation was imperfect, the Scottish Borders fronted the English in three Marches. In the East, where

31

the power of the Homes was great, Fast Castle and Home Castle were the strongholds. In the Middle March Hermitage was the main fastness, and there the houses of the Kerrs were of great importance towards the east, while in the west the Keeper of Liddesdale had a quasi-independent authority. In the West March, which rested on Dumfries and Lochmaben, sometimes a Maxwell, sometimes a Johnstone or a Herries held sway.

On both sides of the Border, the duties of the Wardens were much the same. It was their part to resist invasion during times of war; in peace to prevent smuggling, of horses and cattle particularly, to maintain good justice among their own people and, with the aid of their 'opposite numbers', to administer the Law of the Marches.

Their task was not easy for the 'Law of the Marches' never took the form of a complete code. It was really an accretion of various regulations made by definite treaties between England and Scotland by occasional meetings of Commissioners from both sides, and by a common recognition of customs which had no clear documentary evidence to support them.

The Law was largely concerned with the settlement of local disputes, the giving of oaths, the exchange of pledges, the recovery of stolen cattle, the payment of compensation and so on. It had its gallant side, and the organisation for the 'Day of Law' at which Borderers from both sides of the line should appear, was good. There was a sporting element in the relations of English and Scots. This appears, for example, in the arrangements for the reclaim of stolen cattle; and when the bold Buccleuch, who in 1596 had broken into Carlisle Castle to rescue one of his men, had eventually to surrender his person because his pledges failed him, he deliberately chose as his custodian Robert Carey, then the English Warden of the East March, his great enemy, who treated him handsomely.

Actual slaughters and burnings were perhaps less common than has sometimes been believed, but sometimes ugly work was done. There is some evidence, moreover, that the 'bad men' of one country were sheltered in the other and that the Borderers on both sides of the line shared the sentiment that it was a good thing to avoid official interference with decent ridings and raidings, if this were possible.

The foursquare villages on the south of the line, no less than the peels and bastel houses on the north of it, attest the fact that life on the Borders was often a thing of 'sturt and strife'; but the magical pen of Sir Walter Scott, and the trumpet-blast of the old Ballads upon which he founded many of his writings, have cast over Border history a magic which time cannot remove. Behind the violence and the bloodshed may be traced a spirit of valour and of gay chivalry which survives to the present day.

A mist of memory broods and floats
The Border waters flow
The air is full of ballad notes
Borne out of long ago
Twilight on Tweed—Andrew Lang

THE POETRY AND LEGEND
OF THE BORDER

BY H. L. EDLIN

No part of Great Britain is richer in song and story than the historic
Border, the scene for three hundred years of ordered battle or
irregular affray between two nations sundered by the chances of
history. The Border, unlike so many other national frontiers,
divided politically peoples of the same race and speech. The parti-
sans of both sides wrote in a form of Scots or English that we have
little difficulty in following today. We can therefore all appreciate
the writings from both sides of this ancient boundary. On the
whole the Scots writers were the more prolific, for to them the
Border was a tragic barrier parting them not only from a hostile
England but also from the Continent farther south. To the English,
in easier contact with Europe, the Border lay at the end of things
and so attracted the attention of local rather than national poets.

Much of the early Border poetry was handed down by word of
mouth, until diligent writers such as Sir Walter Scott and Bishop
Percy recorded it in print. So rather than investigate dates and
origins, it will be simpler here to classify it in a general way by the
nature of its theme, citing suitable examples. A point to remember
is that there are often several versions of these poems, and no 'author-
ised version' of any.

First we have the narrative ballad, in which the Border is

particularly rich. Here the whole story is set down by some minstrel present as an eye witness, who related it at some distant time or place. Though the language may strike us as quaint there is an insistence on detail that makes the story still live. The characters of each drama are often introduced casually by their Christian names so that they seem already as well known to us as they were to their contemporaries. Take as an example the opening verse of *Kinmont Willie:*

> O have ye na heard o' the fause Sakelde?
> O have ye na heard o' the keen Lord Scroope?
> How they hae ta'en bauld Kinmont Willie
> On Haribee to hang him up?

But all ended well for that unlucky hero, rescued from the dungeons of Carlisle Castle by 'the bauld Buccleuch', Keeper on the Scottish side, who fled with his band across the flooded Eden:

> He turn'd him on the other side,
> And at Lord Scroope his glove flung he:
> 'If ye like na my visit in merry England,
> In fair Scotland come visit me!'

These events, which are well attested historically, took place in Queen Elizabeth's reign, in A.D. 1596.

Another side of the story appears in the English ballad entitled *The Death of Parcy Reed*, which begins:

> God send the land deliverance
> Frae every reaving, riding Scot;
> We'll sune hae neither cow nor ewe
> We'll sune hae neither staig nor stot.

The ill-fated Reed of Troughend Tower, while hunting the deer of Redesdale, was treacherously deserted by his companions and slain by the Crosiers of Liddesdale with whom he was at feud. The following verse exemplifies the straight-forward accounts of mortal conflict with which these ballads abound:

> They fell upon him all at once,
> They mangled him most cruellie;
> The slightest wound might caused his deid,
> And they hae gi'en him thirty-three;
> They hackit off his hands and feet,
> And left him lying on the lee.

The English were however not always the innocent party. In that well-known story *Jamie Telfer of the Fair Dodhead*, we hear how the Captain of Bewcastle led a raid into Teviotdale:

And when they came to the fair Dodhead
Right hastily they clam the peel;
They loosed the kye out, ane and a',
And ranshackled the hoose right weel.

Two very famous ballads relate incidents in the long-standing
feud between the Percy family of Northumberland, and the Douglases on the Scottish side. One is *Chevy Chase*, wherein the trouble
began because the Percy ventured to hunt deer on Scots territory.
The other is *The Battle of Otterburn*, and both deal with that historic
encounter which took place, in A.D. 1388, on or beside the Forest
Park land. The following verses are drawn from the *Otterburn*
version:

To Newcastle when that they came,
The Douglas cry'd on hyght:
Harry Percy, an thou bidest within,
Come to the field, and fight!

When Percy wi' the Douglas met,
I wat he was fu' fain!
They swakked their swords, till sair they swat,
And the blood ran down like rain.

This fray was fought at Otterbourne,
Between the night and the day;
Earl Douglas was buried at the bracken bush,
And the Percy led captive away.

Among more modern poetry Scott's *Marmion* relates the story of
the battle of Flodden, and its opening lines well recapture the spirit
of those times:

Day set on Norham's castled steep
And Tweed's fair river, broad and deep
And Cheviot's mountains lone;
The battled towers, the Donjon Keep,
The loop-hole grates where captives weep,
The flanking walls that round it sweep
In yellow lustre shone.
The scouts had parted on their search,
The castle gates were barr'd;
Above the gloomy portal arch,
Timing his foot steps to a march,
The warder kept his guard,
Low humming as he paced along,
Some ancient Border gathering song.

Also among the more modern works, though with a fine

traditional flavour, come the marching songs, the calls to arms, the stirring rhythms of advancing armies. What song can make the pulse beat quicker than Scott's *Blue Bonnets*?

> March! March! Ettrick and Teviotdale!
> Why the deil dinna ye march forward in order?
> March! March! Eskdale and Liddesdale!
> A' the blue bonnets are bound for the Border!
> Many a banner spread
> Flutters above your head
> Many a crest that is famous in story!
> Mount and make ready then,
> Sons of the mountain glen,
> Fight for the Queen and the old Scottish glory!

What again could better, for a bold boast on the road to battle, Baroness Nairne's *Hundred Pipers*, with its rousing beat:

> Wi' a hundred pipers an a', an' a',
> Wi' a hundred pipers an a', an' a',
> We'll up an' gie them a blaw, a blaw,
> Wi' a hundred pipers an a', an a'
> Oh! its owre the Border awa', awa',
> It's owre the Border awa', awa',
> We'll on and we'll march to Carlisle ha',
> Wi' its yetts, its castell, an a' an' a'.

After the battle came the reckoning. The Border has its store of laments for the fallen, the best-known being Jean Elliot's *Lament for Flodden*, which commemorates the Scots who fell on that battlefield, and begins:

> I've heard them liltin' at the ewe-milkin',
> Lasses a'-liltin' before dawn o' day,
> Now they are moanin' on ilka green loanin'
> The Flowers o' the Forest are a' wede away.

In a different vein come the few romantic ballads, including the exquisite, traditional *Tam Lin* which is set in the Carterhaugh country on the Roxburghshire side of the Forest Park. It tells how Fair Janet, seduced by an elfin lover, rescues him from the supernatural world of the Queen o' Fairies at a weird midnight tryst of the witches:

> About the dead hour o' the nicht
> She heard the bridles ring
> And Janet was as glad at that
> As any earthly thing

36

> They shaped him in her arms at last
> A mother-naked man
> She cast her mantle over him
> And sae her love she wan.

But often romance is blighted by violent death, and within one ballad one finds a rich mixture of affection and grief, as in *The Douglas Tragedy* which tells how the Lady Margaret, eloping with her Lord William, was pursued by her father and seven brothers. It is characteristic of these stories that nothing ever happens by halves:

> O, there she stood, and bitter she stood
> And never did shed one tear
> Until that she saw her seven brethren fa
> And her father, who lov'd her so dear

But in the conflict Lord William too had suffered a mortal wound:

> Lord William was dead long ere midnight,
> Lady Margaret long ere day,
> And all true lovers that go thegither
> May they have mair luck than they!

Lovers were not always faithful. In the English ballad *The Fair Flower of Northumberland*, the maiden who helped her captured Scots sweetheart to escape is curtly dismissed:

> They rode till they came to a Scottish moss,
> *Follow my love, come over the strand*
> He bade her light off from her father's horse
> Says, 'Go get you back to Northumberland!'

Among the later poems of fancy with a legendary background, perhaps the most remarkable is the *Gloaming Bucht*, written by James Telfer of Jedburgh about 1824, on the basis of local tradition concerning the goblins who haunted Wauchope and the Carter Bar. It tells how 'bonnie Jean Rule' who milked the ewes at the bucht at eventide, was persuaded by her shepherd lover to sing as the light failed.

> The liltings o' that silver voice
> That rose an' fell so free
> They softer were than lover's lute,
> Heard o'er a sleeping sea.

Inevitably the jealous fairies were awakened, and a little green goblin appeared who first raised a yell so shrill that it reached to the stars and sent the moon scurrying behind a cloud. Then he sang 'sae witchingly and sweet' that all the creatures of the wilds came and

fawned upon him, the ewes danced to and fro, and the hapless
Jean Rule swooned:

> It might be glamoury, or not
> In sooth I cannot say,
> It was the witching time of night
> The hour o' gloaming grey
> And she that lay in her loveris armis,
> I wis was a weel-faured may.
> Her pulses all were beating trewe,
> Her heart was louping light,
> Unto that wondrous melody
> That simple song of night.

Jean Rule recovered at length from her trance, but never again
did she dare to raise her beautiful voice in the gloaming amid the
Border hills.

THE LAST FAIRY OF WAUCHOPE FOREST

The following extract from a contribution by Robert White to
the *Local Historian's Table Book*, Legendary Division, Vol. II, P. 137
(1844), relates a story told by Robert Oliver, an old shepherd who
lived at Southdean until about 1830, in the dialect spoken on the
Scottish side of the Border:

'Speakin' o' fairies,' said Robie, 'I can tell you about the verra last
fairy that ever wes seen hereaway. When my faither, Peter Oliver,
was a young man, he lived at Hyndlee and herdit the Brockalaw.
Weel, it was the custom to milk yowes i' thae days, and my faither
was buchtin' the Brockalaw yowes to twae young lish clever hizzies
ae nicht after sunset. Nae little "daffin" and "gabbin", as the sang
sings, gaed on amang the threesome, I' se warrant ye, till at last,
just as it begoud to get faughish derk, my faither chanced to look
alang the lea at the head o' the bucht, and what does he see but a
little wee creaturie, a' clad i' green, and wi' lang hair, yellow as
gowd, hingin' round its shoulders, comin' straight for him . . .'

THE COUT OF KIELDER

A grimmer tale of the supernatural concerns the ill-fated Cout
(meaning 'Colt') of Kielder, a young chieftain who ill-advisedly rode
out into Liddesdale to hunt, and on the way rode three times around
the Kielder Stone in a 'widdershins' direction—that is, contrary to
the course of the sun.

He and his companions then went on to dine with the treacherous
Sir William Soulis, Lord of Liddesdale, at Hermitage Castle. Here
all but the Cout were bewitched and rendered helpless, but protected by magic powers the Cout himself escaped as far as the Liddel

Water. No sword or lance could dint his magic armour, but his pursuers forced him into the stream and held him under until he was drowned, at the spot still called 'The Cout of Kielder's Pool'. Retribution awaited Lord Soulis, for at length he was boiled alive in a cauldron of lead on the summit of the Nine Stane Rig. Local tradition asserts that Hermitage Castle sank one foot into the ground through the sheer weight of wickedness committed there!

Such is the stuff of the Border ballads and poems—strife, sudden death, bravery and comradeship with undercurrents of sadness, magic, and romance. They relate the triumphs and the depths of human experience, and nothing written since in or about this region quite matches them in quality. Here we can give but a brief selection, but details of collections in which they may be found appear in the Guide's bibliography on page 90. The most famous of these are of course Sir Walter Scott's *Minstrelsy of the Scottish Border* and Bishop Percy's *Reliques of Ancient Poetry*, while excellent modern anthologies are *The Oxford Book of Ballads* edited by Sir Arthur Quiller Couch, and the *Golden Treasury of Scottish Poetry*, edited by Hugh Macdiarmid. It is often said that no modern writer can catch the authentic ring of the old ballads, but Will H. Ogilvie came very near it with his *Blades of Harden*, of which a typical verse runs:

> Ho! for the blades of Harden!
>   Ho! for the pikes that cross!
> Ho! for the king of lance and ling
>   —A Scott on the Ettrick moss!
> The rough road runs by the Carter,
>   The white foam creams on the rein
> And aye for the blades of Harden
>   'There will be moonlight again!'

Since this chapter is but an introduction to the delights of the Border landscape, we cannot do better than end with the opening verse of Ogilvie's *The Raiders*:

> Last night a wind from Lammermoor
>   came roaring up the glen
> With the tramp of trooping horses
>   and the laugh of reckless men,
> And struck a mailed hand on the gate,
>   and cried in rebel glee
> 'Come forth! Come forth! my Borderer,
>   and ride the March with me!'

At dusk I flung my knapsack on the heath,
  I made my bracken bed, I supped, and soon
As daylight faded from the glen beneath,
  Cool winds among the firs were rising fast
Stirring the sleeping branches till they cast
  Black limbs athwart the silver moon
         An April Night—George Buchanan Smith

THE BORDER FORESTS

BY H. L. EDLIN

It is evident from the scale and success of the new forests of the
Borders that this region is well suited to the growing of coniferous
trees which produce the softwood timbers so widely used in industry,
building and agriculture. But when this great task was begun there
was little to guide the foresters in their choice of method or tree
species. The operations that the visitor will see today, as the plantations are gradually extended over the hills, are the outcome of
trial and experiment. When, in 1920, this region first attracted the
attention of the newly-established Forestry Commission, it was
virtually treeless. Only scattered clusters of birch or oak scrub
persisted along the sides of occasional cleughs, as relics of once
extensive broadleaved woodland. Some useful pioneer planting had,
however, been carried out by a few landowners, usually in the form
of shelter-belts. Successive Dukes of Northumberland had established woods of Norway spruce and Scots pine around Kielder
Castle, whilst at Muirburnhead, to the west of Newcastleton Forest
in Liddesdale, there was already an extensive young plantation,
mainly of Sitka spruce, on the estate of the Duke of Buccleuch.

Using these woods as a guide, the Forestry Commission began its
work with the acquisition of 3,500 acres at Newcastleton in 1920.

Barking Thinnings in a Spruce Wood

Hauling Poles to the Roadway by Horse and Sledge

Cuthbertson Plough Cutting Turfs and Drains for Tree Planting

Planting a Pine in a Turf; note Plug cut out by Semi-circular Spade

Building a Forest Road

*Transplanting Young Spruce in Wauchope Nursery, with the Ledmore
Lining-out Plough*

Self-sown Scots Pines, in William's Cleugh, up the Scalp Burn, Kielder

Moorland around Seven Linns, Chirdon, North Tynedale

It was not until 1926 that the first land was leased on the Northumberland side of the Border; then 2,000 acres were obtained at Smales, now part of Kielder Forest. As experience in afforestation was gained, it was found prudent to extend the afforestation areas as opportunities arose; the largest single acquisition was in 1932 when 47,000 acres of the Kielder Estate was purchased from the Duke of Northumberland. Gradually there has been built up one of the biggest groups of forests in Britain. These are administered from three separate centres; those forests which are in Scotland are controlled from Dumfries, those in Northumberland from York, and those in Cumberland from Chester. There are of course forest officers stationed in or near each group of forests, while each forest, or each beat in the bigger forests, has its own resident Forester in charge of day-to-day work.

The following schedule sets out, for the sake of completeness, the extent of all the Commission forests that lie within, or beside, both the Border Forest Park and the Northumberland National Park, as shown in the sketch map between pages 64–65. The subsequent account deals mainly with six forests that fall wholly or partly within the Border Forest Park, namely Kielder, Wark, Redesdale, Kershope, Newcastleton and the main portion of Wauchope; similar work is, however, being done at all the Border Forests.

Area in acres

Forest	Total Area	Area under Trees 1960	Area to be planted	Area used for grazing etc.
1. *Border Forests in Northumberland under the North-East England Conservancy, York*				
Kielder	72,354	45,239	2,761	24,354
Wark	36,448	23,052	1,079	12,317
Redesdale	17,252	12,056	109	5,087
Kidland	3,806	2,597	1,076	133
Harwood	8,343	7,700	—	643
Chillingham	986	847	115	24
Rothbury	4,163	3,246	542	375
	143,352	94,737	5,682	42,933
2. *Border Forests in Cumberland under the North-West England Conservancy, Chester*				
Kershope	11,407	9,688	81	1,638
Spadeadam	10,287	4,100	2,968	3,219
Longtown	637	350	287	—
	22,331	14,138	3,336	4,857

41

		Area in acres		
Forest	Total Area	Area under Trees 1960	Area to be planted	Area used for grazing etc.
3. Border Forests in Roxburghshire and Dumfries-shire, under the South Scotland Conservancy, Dumfries				
Newcastleton	7,754	5,891	1,473	309
Wauchope	13,495	7,996	1,391	4,108
	21,249	13,887	2,864	4,498
Grand Total for three Conservancies	186,932	122,762	11,882	52,288

Altogether there are 187,000 acres of land, or nearly 300 square miles, comprised in this Border Forest Group. Of this some 126,000 acres fall within the Border Forest Park, 50,000 acres fall within the Northumberland National Park, and 13,000 acres lie closely adjacent. The two areas wholly excluded from the two National Parks, namely Spadeadam Forest and the Leithope section of Wauchope, are remotely situated and have at present little to attract the visitor.

The guiding spirit of the great Border afforestation scheme was the late Lord Robinson, who began his forestry career in 1909, and was the Chairman of the Forestry Commission from 1932 to 1952. On his elevation to the peerage in 1947, he took his territorial title: 'of Kielder Forest in the County of Northumberland and Adelaide in the Commonwealth of Australia', in part from the great new forest that he had done so much to create, and in part from his birthplace. Having witnessed the planting of the first trees at Smales in 1926, he returned, in 1948, to fell the first trees that had grown large enough, during the intervening 22 years, to be removed in the thinning of the oldest plantation.

When he died in 1952 his ashes were scattered among the trees he loved, and a memorial cairn at Whickhope, deep in Kielder Forest, records his great work for the Border woodlands, which themselves provide his finest memorial.

Let us now look at the operations carried out to form and tend these young forests. As yet these are mainly concerned with the establishment phase, or with the harvesting of poles culled from the young stands when thinnings are made, for none of the trees planted by the Commission is more than forty-one years old. Ahead lies the yield of the mature timber, when the trees have reached an age of sixty to eighty years; only then will the full productivity of the woods become manifest. At that stage, it is proposed to avoid any large clear fellings, but rather to clear the crop in small groups or sections, and perhaps to secure a fresh crop from the seedlings of the mature trees.

PREPARING THE GROUND

Each year, at each of the several Border Forests, the tract of land selected, as indicated in the management scheme, is made ready for the following season's planting; it may be as much as 1,000 acres in extent. First the forest staff prepare a plan showing where the main roads or tracks will run, and the courses of the streams or main drainage channels. To this they add rides and fire-breaks, which help to break the area up into portions of about twenty-five acres in extent, known as compartments. Each compartment is then ploughed, using a huge hill drainage plough pulled by a powerful crawler tractor, to cut furrows spaced five feet apart. At the same time it provides continuous strips of turf on which the young trees will later be planted.

In the early days the young trees were planted directly into the surface of the peaty soil, but when so treated they grew very slowly and sometimes failed. Research showed the way to better results obtainable by cutting drainage channels with hand tools, and planting the trees on the resultant turfs. This method made heavy demands on labour but thousands of acres were successfully afforested in this way. Then it was found that tractor-drawn ploughs could be used to get the same or better results more quickly and cheaply. Ploughing is used for various purposes at different forests, but here in the peaty soil on the Borders its object is to improve drainage and provide turfs.

After the ploughing, the drainage network is completed by special drainage ploughs or else by hand. Then the planting area is securely fenced against sheep, usually with wide-mesh sheep netting; rabbit netting, which is essential at many forests, has not been found necessary here in the Borders.

CHOOSING THE TREES

The bulk of the land being afforested in the Borders is planted with spruces, which are easy to establish and promise to give high yields on peaty soils in a region of fairly high rainfall. Norway spruce, which has green needles set singly on little pegs along its

43

twigs, and is familiar to everyone as the Christmas tree, is selected for much of the lower ground; for it is fairly resistant to the frost that occur there in late spring. Higher up the hills, Sitka spruce which comes from Alaska and British Columbia and has bluish-green sharp-tipped needles, likewise borne on pegs, is preferred, because although it is frost-tender in the spring it is more resistant to strong winds. On the more grassy peats the spruces promise the quickest growth and highest yield, but they do not thrive as a pure crop on the heathery ground; there pines are used, either the native Scots pine with its blue-green needles set in pairs, or the rather similar but hardier lodgepole pine, with dull green foliage, which comes from Washington or British Columbia. Often the lodgepole pine is intermixed with Sitka spruce to nurse that up, since the spruce yields more timber. When there is bracken amid the natural vegetation, the Japanese larch, which has little tufts of bluish-green needles that fall each winter leaving the russet twigs bare, is found to thrive; it grows quickly and yields timber with a durable heartwood, suitable for rustic work, pit props, and farm fencing. As the young larches do not themselves burn readily, and as they soon suppress inflammable growth below them, they are also found useful as living fire breaks.

These five coniferous trees account for nearly all the new afforestation in the Borders, but wherever better ground is found other trees are introduced, with the object of diversifying the plantations and their produce. These include hardwoods such as beech and oak, and some of the less common conifers such as hemlock, Lawson cypress, Douglas fir, Serbian spruce and two silver firs, *Abies grandis* and *Abies procera*, from North Western America.

RAISING YOUNG TREES FOR PLANTING

Practically all the small trees used for planting are raised from seed in the Commission's own nurseries in or near the Border country. In detail, these are:

Widehaugh Nursery, 69 acres, on the main Newcastle—Carlisle road, 2 miles east of Hexham.

Kershope Nursery, 27 acres, beside Kershopefoot Station in Liddesdale.

Wauchope Nurseries, 33 acres; main nursery near Bonchester Bridge, smaller one at Swinney.

To give an idea of the scale of work involved, the Widehaugh Nursery employs forty people, and produces, each year, about 7 *million* trees. Because the methods used in the Borders, involving the careful preparation of the site by ploughing before planting, enable a rather small tree to be used, the nurseries are not very spectacular to the casual visitor; but much exacting work goes on there. From the small seeds of the conifers the foresters aim to raise, in one or two seasons, a tree seedling big enough to merit transplanting to another nursery bed. Millions of these seedlings, each only a few inches high, are transplanted or lined out each spring, to grow on in fertile ground. When they are from eighteen months to four years old in all, they are from one to two feet tall, and have developed bushy root systems that will give them a good start on the exposed hillsides. These small transplants are relatively cheap to raise, and a very high proportion take root successfully.

PLANTING THE NEW WOODS

During the winter and early spring, a steady supply of young trees is sent from the nurseries to the planting grounds by lorry; they may complete their journey on a trailer or even on a sledge drawn by a tractor. Then they are passed over to the planting gangs, each member of which carries a planting bag, slung from his shoulder, to hold a supply of trees. Although planting is done at great speed, and 1,500 trees per man per day is quite a common figure, nearly every tree takes root. Two planting methods are used. One, which is seldom seen outside the Borders, consists of cutting a circular hole in the prepared turf with a peculiar long-handled tool rather like a bulb planter, called a semi-circular spade. The other, more widely known, method of turf planting, involves the cutting of a slit through the turf with a spade, so that the tree's roots can be set between the two layers of turf where the plough 'slice' meets the unbroken ground. At a spacing of five feet apart each way, 1,500 trees are needed for each acre of land, after allowing for the space left for rides, etc. Hence a planting programme of 1,000 acres a year requires at least 1½ *million* young trees annually.

TENDING AND PROJECTING THE PLANTATIONS

Because of the thorough ground preparation, the young plantations do not need much weeding, but the growth of grass or bracken around the young trees must be cut down with a reaping hook in the summer, for the first year or two. Thereafter the trees raise their leading shoots clear of weeds, and need no further help. For the next twelve or fifteen years, the forester has only to protect them against fire or other possible perils. His fences must be well maintained, to keep out stray sheep, and roe deer, hares, and wild goats have to be kept under control. Young plantations at this stage seldom suffer seriously from insects or fungal diseases.

Fire, however, is always at the back of the forester's mind, for both the young trees themselves and the grass, bracken and heather amid which they grow are highly inflammable during dry weather. The worst season for fire risk is the spring, when conditions are nearly always very dry. Elaborate precautions have been taken to reduce the risk of loss, and the visitor can do much to help here by always realising that unguarded sources of fire, whether they be matches, cigarette ends, or picnic fires, could readily involve the Border Forest Park in a major calamity. In Kielder's worst fire, at Chirdon in 1947, no less than 700 acres of valuable young plantations were completely destroyed in a few hours. The forest staff are determined to ensure that such a loss shall not happen again.

Along the main road up the North Tyne valley, you will see narrow grazing strips of improved grass fringing the plantations; here sheep and cattle keep the herbage short and fireproof.

Other obvious signs of fire protection arrangements are the towers or look-out cabins erected on the hills giving the best viewpoints. These are constantly manned during dry weather, by watchers linked by telephone with the fire control centre for each forest. At the fire control centre a warden or forester is continually on duty, and as soon as suspicious smoke is reported by one tower, he finds out its exact source by getting a cross-bearing from another tower. Standing by are his fire-fighting vehicles, specially equipped Land Rovers or lorries, with a trained crew within call. A short-wave radio installation enables the fire duty officer to keep in touch with watch towers and vehicles, wherever they may happen to be in the forest. Within minutes of a fire being reported, pumps, water supplies, and fire-fighters will be speeding to the scene, for prompt action is essential if a small fire is to be put out before it can develop into a big blaze. Arrangements exist, of course, for calling in county fire services and troops, but the Border foresters always aim to get each fire under control before reinforcements are needed.

The visitor will note how well the forest has been split up by firebreaks and roads, which give ready access and provide base-lines along which a spreading fire may be checked. He will also see, at intervals along the roadside, stacks of fire brooms ready for volunteer fire-fighters to seize in order to beat out a fire at once, and give it no chance to spread. Should one find a small fire breaking out the best thing to do is to grab a beater and attack it at once; it is surprising how much good a few determined people with beaters can accomplish. If there are several people in the party, then one should promptly be despatched to give warning to the Foresters or Fire Services (Dial 100).

Take heed, too, of the bold signs that show, from day to day, the degree of fire danger intensity in the forests, notably along the main road from Otterburn to Carter Bar.

Before afforestation began, this region was virtually roadless; only an occasional cart track led from one of the very few main roads to some isolated farmstead. A good road system is essential for proper forest management, at first for quick access for tree planting and fire protection, and later also for the hauling out of the poles and timber cut in the woods. The Commission's engineers are therefore engaged on a big programme of road construction, involving also the building of bridges, which will eventually make every part of the plantations accessible to motor transport. These gravel roads are simple and economical, but adequate for their purpose. Most of the gravel is dug from the beds of hill streams.

The roads are not open to visitors' cars, which would be liable to hinder the essential work of fire protection and timber haulage; but walkers are free to use them at most times of the year. Occasionally, however, at periods of extreme fire risk, it may be necessary to impose some restrictions.

THE HARVEST OF THE THINNINGS

The young plantations of conifers will take from sixty to eighty years to reach full maturity, and only gradually will timber of the larger sizes become available from the woods. Meanwhile, big intermediate yields are obtained from the woods in their younger stages and these may be equal in sum to the long-awaited final crop. From fifteen to twenty-five years after planting, the young trees crowd one another so closely that some thinning out becomes essential if the better specimens are to develop properly. So the forester cuts out a due proportion, often about one fifth of their number. Thinning is a skilled operation which may be done by various methods, but the guiding principle is always to preserve the best trees, which will prove the most valuable, to the last. Thinnings have to be repeated at intervals varying from three to ten years, according to the rate of growth of the crop; eventually, only about one tree in every eight, of those originally planted, will be left to attain its full size. Before the first thinning is done, the lower branches must be pruned from some or all of the trees, in the process known as 'brashing'; this improves access, lessens fire risk, and aids the formation of better timber with fewer knots.

After each tree selected for removal has been marked by the forester, the fellers come and rapidly bring it down with axe and saw. Then they trim away the branches and often strip off the bark with a draw-knife or barking spade. Then the trimmed log is drawn out to the roadside; despite the many mechanical devices that have been tried for short hauls, the best and cheapest way to move it at this stage is still by means of a horse. So useful are these sturdy horses, that it has been found worth while to use horse-boxes, towed by a Land Rover, to save time in taking them out to their haulage work in the woods.

At the roadside, the log may be barked on a mechanical peeler, and then cross-cut on a small portable, power-driven sawbench into short lengths, according to the purposes in view. The material is then despatched by lorry to the consumers.

The work outlined here is sometimes done by the Forestry Commission's own staff, and sometimes by men employed by timber merchants who buy the marked trees as they stand, for conversion to pit props or planks either in the forest or at the sawmill.

Thinning has been in progress for several years at the older-established Border forests, such as Kershope and Newcastleton; it is getting under way at Kielder and Redesdale, and eventually Wark and Wauchope will add to the yield of thinning material. An area of some 135,000 acres under plantation means that ultimately about 35,000 acres must be thinned each year, so it is clear that the annual output will be very considerable. Each acre of plantation can be expected to grow at least 100 hoppus feet of timber each year; this hoppus foot is the forester's customary measure and is equivalent to some $1\frac{1}{4}$ true cubic feet of round timber; it weighs, when freshly felled, about 75 lbs. Roughly half the annual growth will be removed in the form of thinnings, and the rest will be final crop timber. The thinnings alone will gradually reach a total of 6 million hoppus feet, or about 200,000 tons, of material to be harvested and despatched each year. The values cannot be forecast with equal accuracy, for the prices realised vary considerably with the quality and stage of preparation of the material. But at present levels it can be foreseen that the monetary return from thinnings alone will be of the order of £$1\frac{1}{2}$ million a year. These are the prospective yields that encouraged foresters to embark on this large-scale afforestation project. Now let us see how the timber is used in the national economy.

The bigger trees removed in thinnings are already large enough for sawing into boxboards, and logs for this purpose are sent to Washington near Newcastle. As time goes on, sawn timber of larger sizes, to serve more varied purposes, will become available. Sawmills will probably be set up within the Forest Park providing further local employment. Spruce, the main timber grown, is suitable for joinery, box-making, and many other purposes, and large quantities are regularly imported under the name of Baltic whitewood or white deal.

48

The straighter poles make good pitprops; they are barked and cut to specified lengths and diameters to suit the various coal seams. Two coalfields are within easy reach, namely the big Northumberland coalfied and the West Cumberland one. Scottish coalfields in Lanarkshire and Midlothian can also be supplied. When it is considered that, in the past, these pits relied almost entirely on props imported from Northern Europe, the advantage to the nation of having a home-grown source of supply on the very verge of the coalfields, will be realised; clearly it renders our sources of coal, and so of power, both cheaper and more secure.

There are local demands from farmers for fencing stakes and rails, but these are being met from the smaller stuff, and more distant industrial outlets are coming into being. Recently a chipboard factory has been set up by a commercial firm at Annan in Dumfries-shire, to use some of the small thinnings in the manufacture of a useful building and furniture material which enjoys a wide demand. Another chipboard factory is in operation at Stockton-on-Tees and yet another near Newcastle. Tree tops for making hardboard, another building material, have been sent as far as Queensferry in North Wales. Spruce wood, which forms the bulk of the harvest, is a good timber for paper pulp, and substantial amounts already go to a big newsprint mill at Ellesmere Port in Cheshire. The manufacture of wood wool, a packing material, at a Yorkshire factory, also absorbs some of the current output.

Other products of the thinning operations are telegraph poles, small poles for tripods for drying hay or corn, and rustic poles for gardens. Uses have even been investigated for the bark which is stripped away; it holds tannins suitable for treating leather.

Thus the productive purpose of the Border Forests extends beyond their immediate surroundings to distant industrial centres. The most encouraging feature of their output is its organisation on a basis of sustained yield; the woods will continue to yield at the rates forecast, far into the future, as one tree crop succeeds another.

EMPLOYMENT

It is not a simple matter to estimate the amount of employment provided by the Border Forests, for the direct employment under the Forestry Commission accounts for only part of it; other people work for timber merchants, haulage contractors, or in distant factories. Moreover, the thinning programme is only gradually getting under way. The current total for the six forests of Kielder, Wark, Redesdale, Kershope, Newcastleton and Wauchope is around 500 people directly employed; most, but not all, of them now live in the new forest villages. For the future, it is perhaps best to think in terms of one man at work in every 100 acres of woodlands, with another man engaged on various stages of preparing and hauling out their produce. Thus, for 135,000 acres of plantations, some 2,700 workers will be required; allowing for their families, this means at least 7,500 people drawing their livelihood directly from the Border forests. Past records show that, before afforestation began, these hills supported only a few hundred people engaged on shepherding or gamekeeping.

A SCHOOL FOREST PLOT

In Newcastleton Forest, the old steading called Kershope, beside the Kershope Burn, has been set aside as a school forest plot. Here the senior pupils from the Newcastleton Junior Secondary School study forestry and natural history, using the old cottage as their base. In all, ten acres of land are available for instructional purposes. Six acres are gradually being planted up by the scholars of successive years. The remaining four acres carries plantations, and here the boys select trees for thinning out, fell them, and cut them up into useful sizes.

Grass-heads, drooping on their stems,
Wear a thousand spherèd gems;
And from the foxglove's freckled lip
Distillations drip and drip;
Beaded bluebells, frail and fine,
Have ta'en a fill of rainy wine:
    So all those blooms in thriftless beauty flowing
        Which of the waste are claim'd
    With milfoil, meadowsweet and kingcups growing
        Nameless or never named

—Sir George Douglas

THE VEGETATION OF
THE PARK

BY DR. W. A. CLARK

Topographically the park consists of a deeply dissected plateau, the greater part of which lies more than 700 feet above sea level. Much of it exceeds 1,000 feet in altitude and in places, particularly in the north of the area, it closely approaches the 2,000-foot contour. The annual rainfall as recorded at Kielder (633 feet in altitude) amounts to some forty-five to fifty inches, but on the higher ground this figure must be considerably exceeded.

The whole of the area with the exception perhaps of some of the higher hills is blanketed with Boulder Clay. Although the nature of this Boulder Clay varies considerably, the general tendency is for the sand fraction to be high. It is not surprising, therefore, taking also into consideration the relatively high average annual rainfall of the area, that leached acid soils prevail over much of the Forest Park region. The main vegetational types are thus those

51

characteristic of upland acid soils and, while these communities are not floristically very rich in species, they are not without interest to the botanist.

On the better drained soils, heather (*Calluna*) often occurs abundantly, accompanied by such species as cowberry (*Vaccinium vitis-idaea*), crowberry (*Empetrum*) and more rarely the common clubmoss (*Lycopodium clavatum*). Among the rocks of the sandstone outcrops the rare climbing fumitory (*Corydalis claviculata*) may also be found. Such drained soils, when not too base-deficient, conform to the brown earth soil type and support bent-fescue grasslands with sheep's fescue (*Festuca ovina*) and the bent grasses (*Agrostis* spp.) as the dominant plants. The flora of these upland pastures can be relatively rich, with the sweet vernal-grass (*Anthoxanthum*), the decumbent heath-grass (*Sieglingia*), tormentil, the field and heath wood-rushes, devil's-bit scabious, the heath bedstraw, lousewort, eyebright, milkwort, and the pill-headed sedge (*Carex pilulifera*) as representative species. Heather, characteristic of this community, is kept in abeyance by grazing, and only shows itself plainly after the sheep have been fenced out to permit of tree planting.

By far the most abundant type of grassland, however, in the Park area is that dominated by the purple moor-grass (*Molinia*). This grassland is characteristic of damper soil, the surface of which is generally covered with a layer of peat of varying depth, formed partly from the dead remains of the *Molinia* itself. The composition of this community varies considerably from place to place, but heather, the cross-leaved heath (*Erica tetralix*), the bilberry (*Vaccinium myrtillus*), the cotton grass (*Eriophorum vaginatum*), the crowberry, the heath spotted-orchid (*Orchis ericetorum*), the wavy hair-grass, the deer grass or sedge (*Trichophorum caespitosum*), and the ribbed sedge (*Carex binervis*), may be taken as fairly representative of this type of vegetation. Where slightly drier conditions prevail, particularly during the summer months, the moor mat-grass (*Nardus*) may become dominant, accompanied by the heath rush (*Juncus squarrosus*). These grasslands and the heather moors now provide the principal areas for afforestation, and as the light-excluding tree canopy develops, much of this vegetation, except perhaps in the rides where *Molinia* continues to flourish, will ultimately disappear.

Extensive areas on the fell tops where the soil is waterlogged and permanently wet, are covered with peat moss vegetation of some kind. Such soils are characteristically blue-grey in colour due to the fact that the iron salts, in the absence of oxygen, are in the *ferrous* condition. They are known as *gley* soils. Much of the peat is relatively shallow, varying from eighteen inches or less up to six feet in depth, and it conforms to the blanket bog type. But in the deeper basins peat over twenty feet in depth may be found. The vegetation of these peaty areas varies considerably and depends largely on the extent to which it has been modified by man through drainage, heather burning and grazing by sheep and cattle. Several very good examples of peat moss vegetation, relatively undamaged by man, occur in the area lying between the Chirdon Burn—a tributary of the North Tyne—and the Roman Wall to the south. A particularly fine example is to be found near Hope House at the head of the Chirdon. Here the dominant plant is the bog moss (*Sphagnum*), represented by several species which form a complete, more or less uniform cover over the surface of the bog. The principal plants growing in the sphagnum mat are *Calluna*, the cotton grasses (*Eriophorum angustifolium* and *E. vaginatum*), bog asphodel, cross-leaved heath, cranberry, the bog rosemary (*Andromeda*), the round and long-leaved sundews (*Drosera rotundifolia* and *D. anglica*) and the deer grass or sedge. The bog rosemary is a particularly lovely plant, characteristic of relatively undisturbed bogs in the north of England, and is therefore a rare plant. The occurrence of *Drosera anglica* is also of special interest because this is now the only known station for this plant in Northumberland and Durham. Two interesting sedges, *Carex curta* and *C. limosa*, occur in the vicinity of this moss. Both are again found on Falstone Moss but the latter is very rare indeed. Here then, we have an exceptionally good example of a still actively growing moss with a complete and healthy cover of *Sphagnum*. There is now every hope that this moss will never be drained and that its vegetation will be preserved for posterity.

The draining and burning of peat mosses, and to a lesser extent the treading and grazing by animals, result in the disappearance of bog moss and the smaller species growing in it and tend, therefore, to favour the dominance of the larger species, particularly the sheathed cotton-grass (*Eriophorum vaginatum*). In June, when this cotton grass is in flower, these drained mosses look as if covered with snow and stand out conspicuously on the hills even from long distances. Sheep are very fond of the cotton-grass early in the season and pull the young flowering shoots out of their basal sheaths—hence the local name of 'draw moss' for this plant. A feature of all these moorland areas deserving special mention is the vivid colour of the vegetation when seen in the late autumn in the yellowing evening sun—the range of colour varying from red through orange to several shades of brown.

The peat mosses are not only of interest to the botanist for the *present* vegetation they support but also because, locked up in the peat, is the history of the development of the surrounding vegetation since the time the peat started to form. All bog species contribute to the formation of peat but by far the most important plant in this respect is the bog moss. As new shoots of this plant continue to be formed on the surface of the bog the older parts below die and, as decay is prevented by lack of oxygen and by acid conditions, the dead remains are preserved and eventually become compacted to form peat. In this way, as long as a living cover of *Sphagnum* survives, the moss grows in height. Also preserved in the developing peat are pollen grains derived from the plants of the peat vegetation itself and from forest trees growing in the neighbourhood of the moss. Thus, if samples are taken from different levels in the peat and treated to reveal their pollen content, the nature of the vegetation, both of the peat moss and the surrounding area, can be determined for any given stage in the history of the moss. From a peat boring carried out on Falstone Moss (850 feet) by Dr. Kathleen Blackburn of King's College, Newcastle-upon-Tyne, it was determined that the peat, 20 feet in depth, started to form after the Ice Age some 8,000 years ago during the late Boreal period. At this time open birch forest with some Scots pine was present in the area and the stumps of some of these pines can still be seen on Falstone Moss where they have been exposed by erosion and by the burning of the peat, following a moor fire at the end of the 18th century. With the improvement of the climate, pine became more abundant and hazel increased dramatically in amount. Soon warmth-demanding trees appeared, here represented by elm and oak.

During the ensuing Atlantic period pine and birch decreased in amount and oak became more abundant. Lime made its appearance at this stage and alder became increasingly common but surprisingly, unlike birch, remains of its wood are seldom found in the peat. It would therefore seem that the alder as at the present day was confined to the wetter areas in the valley bottoms. The climate was now at its most favourable—the so called Post-Glacial Climatic Optimum. Forests of the type developed during this climatic optimum persisted for some 5,000 years but during the latter part of this period the climate became drier. Then about 500 B.C. a marked climatic deterioration took place and conditions again became wetter. This is reflected in an increase in the amount of heather, grass and sedge pollen in the peat relative to the amount of tree pollen, thus indicating a decrease in the extent of the forest. Furthermore, in the woodlands which remained, birch, hazel and alder became more abundant again at the expense of oak. Simultaneously, the bogs became wetter and a period of rapid bog building by *Sphagnum* ensued.

This outline of forest development in the Post-Glacial period determined from Falstone Moss is essentially similar to that based on examination of peat from Broadgate Fell and Wellhaugh Flow, both of which also occur in the Forest Park. In its general features the forest development, as outlined above, agrees with that for England as a whole. Dr. Blackburn has, however, clearly demonstrated that in the Forest Park, and probably in the whole of North-East England, birch and hazel were at all times more abundant than elsewhere in England; on the other hand oak was at no time as plentiful in the Park as in more lowland situations.

This brings us to early historic times when the Forest Park area was characterised by very much reduced forests of birch, hazel and alder. From then to the present day man must be held chiefly responsible for the almost complete disappearance of natural woodland in the area. Grazing which prevented regeneration, together with a certain amount of felling for timber, have been the principal factors responsible, although long continued leaching of the soil may also have played a part. Today only relics of the original forests survive on the steep sides of sheltered valleys and gullies where sheep have been unable to graze. Examples of this relict woodland can be found here and there on the banks of small streams running into the North Tyne. Birch is usually the dominant tree in these woodlands but rowan and occasionally the common ash are also present. In the wetter areas near the streams alder is frequent; several species of willow and the bird cherry are also quite characteristic of these wet situations. Hazel and hawthorn occur occasionally in the sparse shrub layer. The soils are generally of the brown earth type, leached but not as acid as on adjoining moorland.

A good example of this relict woodland is to be found on the banks of a small stream running through Falstone, where the field layer is surprisingly rich in species. The creeping soft-grass (*Holcus mollis*) is the dominant plant but gives way to the wavy hair-grass on the shallower soils where the shales outcrop. Accompanying these grasses are the wood sorrel, the earthnut, tormentil, the hairy woodrush and more rarely the wood crane's-bill, greater stitchwort, wood anemone, foxglove, wood-sage, strawberry, hedge woundwort, primrose, the greater woodrush and herb Robert. The wetter areas are characterised by valerian, marsh hawk's-beard (*Crepis paludosa*), meadow-sweet, lesser celandine, wild angelica, marsh thistle, water avens and wood horsetail. The ferns include the mountain shield fern (*Thelypteris oreopteris*) and the oak fern. The green hellebore (*Helleborus viridis*) has been found in Ravenshill Wood but may well be a relic of cultivation.

Running practically through the middle of the Forest Park area is the valley of the North Tyne—one of the beauty spots of Northumberland. Here the lush pastures of the alluvial flats or haughs and the wooded banks of the river provide visitors, interested in wild plants, with great opportunities for study. Perhaps the most interesting plant to be found here is the melancholy thistle with its single purple inflorescence and its silver backed leaves but it is really invidious to select one plant from so many. Marsh marigolds, meadow-sweet, meadow-vetchling, the greater burnet, devil's-bit scabious, meadow and wood crane's-bills, figwort, ladies' and greater bedstraws, garlic, mimulus, etc., all contribute to the blaze of colour seen here in the summer. The specialist studying sedges will also find much to interest him in the riverside area and one wet pasture near Falstone yields at least a dozen species. A noteworthy feature in the valley area is the occurrence of large islands in the river which have been formed from debris carried down by the side streams when in flood. Several of these support small alder woods and in the pools which occur in some of them, the alternate-flowered water-milfoil (*Myriophyllum alterniflorum*) flowers prolifically.

Earlier on reference was made to the fact that the greater part of the Park's bedrock carries a deposit of Boulder Clay. Here and there, however, where the thicker limestones outcrop, a fertile base-rich soil is produced. The vegetation of these areas can easily be picked out because of its bright green colour. The dominant species here are the grasses, sheep's fescue, red fescue, and meadow-grass (*Poa pratensis*) but other species indicative of relatively base-rich soils occur such as the quaking-grass, tufted hair-grass (in the wetter areas), the perennial oat-grass (*Helictotrichon pratense*), golden oat-grass (*Trisetum flavescens*), purging flax (*Linum catharticum*), ladies' bedstraw, germander speedwell, tufted vetch (*Vicia cracca*), bird's foot trefoil, harebell, mouse-ear hawkweek (*Hieracium pilosella*) and rough hawkbit (*Leontodon hispidus*).

Areas flushed or watered by streamlets in the vicinity of the limestone sometimes yield the insectivorous butterwort with its lovely blue-spurred flowers, the beautiful Grass of Parnassus, the marsh violet and the lesser clubmoss (*Selaginella selaginoides*). In one such area, at an altitude of 900 feet, dwarf stunted specimens of the common reed (*Phragmites communis*) are to be found.

Lying just behind the southern boundary of the Forest Park is the basaltic outcrop of the whin sill on which is built Hadrian's Wall. Forming as it does a conspicuous landmark, rising to a height of 700 feet above sea level, which is visible from a large part of the forest, a short account of its most interesting botanical features does not seem out of place here. Perhaps the best known botanical station on the wall is that of Crag Lough where, on its southern shore, the basaltic crags rise vertically to a height of over 100 feet. Part of this out-crop is planted with conifers but amongst the large

Curlew's Nest with Chick and Eggs

Short-eared Owl and Chick

Wild Goats

Roe Deer Fawn

The Forest Road down the Lewis Burn, Mounces, Kielder

Bells Linn, Kielder. The Border follows Bells Burn downstream to this point, then strikes up to the right; left and foreground, England; background, Scotland

Pools on the Lewis Burn, near Kielder Camp

Crag Lough and the Whin Sill looking east, Wark Forest

rocks is to be found the mossy saxifrage as well as a rich flora of mosses and liverworts. Further west, in the open amongst the rock talus of the cliffs, a close search reveals the parsley fern and the clubmoss (*Lycopodium selago*)—both locally common elsewhere but very rare species in Northumberland. On more stable regions, the rock rose is often to be found. The lough provides a very rich flora of pond-weeds and at its western end a fen type of vegetation yields the rare *Carex filiformis*. Fringing its shores at the east end is a good example of the willow carrs which are a striking feature of the loughs in this area. The bay willow (*Salix pentandra*) and the tea-leaved willow (*S. phylicifolia*) are the principal species, the former when its fruits burst late in the summer, looking as if covered with snow. The marestail, bog bean, marsh cinquefoil, the smooth horsetail and the reed-grass are also found here. Apart from the richness of its flora, the visitor will find much to interest him at Crag Lough and will be able to see one of the finest stretches of the Roman Wall.

This brief outline of the flora of the Forest Park area does no more than pinpoint the principal features of interest and although the higher alpines of some of the other Scottish Forest Parks are missing, there is much to be seen in the way of compensation. It is very much to be hoped that all who visit the area will do everything they can to protect the flora and thus enable those who come after to enjoy what is part of our national heritage.

Bibliography:

BLACKBURN, KATHLEEN B.

A Long Pollen Diagram from Northumberland. *Trans. Northern Naturalist' Union*, Vol. 11, Pt. 1, 1953.

The midges dance aboon the burn,
  The dews begin to fa
The pairtricks, down the rushy holm,
  Set up their e'ening ca,
Now loud and clear the blackbird's sang
Rings thro the briery shaw;
While flitting gay, the swallows play
  Around the castle wa
          —Robert Tannahill

THE WILD ANIMAL LIFE OF THE BORDER FORESTS

BY ERNEST BLEZARD

Throughout many changes in its long history, the Borderland remains a land of extreme contrasts. Its features alter from sternly wild uplands and bleak wastes to pastures and cultivated land, to the fair settings of villages and hamlets, and to tree-lined river valleys, tranquil in their beauty. Then there are several small lakes to lend a distinctive touch to the scene. And now, where only a place name remains to mark a former birch grove, or an old veteran pine or two to tell of vanished pinewoods, have come the new conifer plantations. This most recent change combines directly with the ancient and old features to increase the richly varied tally of wild animal life.

The afforestation has proved favourable to the increase and spread of certain species and, of mammals affected in this way, the roe deer is an outstanding example. By the end of last century the indigenous roe had apparently become scarce. Later, in the nineteen-twenties, it began to show some recovery from its previous

58

low ebb in both Cumberland and Northumberland. This recovery coincided with the provision of new shelter by the masses of birch scrub which sprang up after the clear felling of so many woodlands during the 1914–18 period. At any time the roe is a wanderer, whether in search of a mate, food or sanctuary, and it would seem likely that the present relatively high population in the harbourage of the young forests had its beginnings in the aftermath of war; numbers are now controlled by planned stalking.

It is a long span since red deer were last hunted in these hills, but there remain the wild goats whose ancestors would see the passing of the deer. Though not true natives, these goats have maintained their wild footing on the exposed heights for a time beyond reckoning. This feral race, often massively horned, assumes a grandeur when, by good fortune, it is seen on The Cheviot itself, or about the arresting crags crowning the skyline of Christianbury and in the hills bordering the forests of Wauchope, Newcastleton and Kielder.

Another naturalised resident, but a later comer, the mountain hare, has a range similar to that of the goats. Some of these blue hares, as they are otherwise known, were introduced from the Highlands fifty years ago. About half a century still earlier, numbers of them were introduced into the south of Scotland where they became widespread. Those now in the forests either spring directly from the later introduction or come as wanderers from the hilly expanses immediately to the north. An occasional individual may get as far down as the Gilsland moors and be strikingly conspicuous in its white winter coat when there is no snow on the ground. At this level the mountain hare may overlap in range with the brown hare, the true native, which lopes from the haughs to the marginal land and beyond. At least a few rabbits have survived the onslaught of myxomatosis, sure indications being given by track-patterned snow.

The red squirrel remains in the older woodlands, especially to the eastern side, in Lower Coquetdale and about Rothbury, and has begun to appear in the Kielder plantations of spruces which have reached the age of cone-bearing. The smaller rodents are further represented by the water voles in their varied aquatic haunts, and by the field voles, the most numerous of all the mammals and most vitally important to so many other wild creatures. In their fluctuating abundance they form the chief prey of the carnivorous birds, the stoats and the weasels. The stoat incidentally, here on occasion partially or almost entirely assumes a white winter coat like that of the northern ermine, a change not necessarily timed by exceptionally wintry conditions.

There are already reports of the rare pine marten, a tree-haunting weasel able to catch squirrels, appearing in the Kershope region.

The little field voles, again, provide many a morsel for the fox, an old, widespread and firmly established resident, equal to picking up a living anywhere and under any conditions. With larger game in view, it is given to raiding the water fowl on those waters which are 'loughs' on the English side of the Border and 'lochs' on the Scottish. There is the lowland fox of the coverts in the main valleys and the hardy hill fox of the wild uplands, which are simply the same species with rather different ways of life, or maybe different home preferences. Most of the crags and broken rock jumbles hold a lair and it is in such places that the hill cubs are born. During the balmy seasons an old fox can occasionally be seen from above curled round like a kitten as he basks out on a sun-warmed rock slab below, in one of these retreats.

The badger and the roe deer are closely linked by association. Both are animals of ancient British lineage and both have recovered from greatly reduced numbers, if not from the 'verge of extinction', to become common and widespread over very much the same ground, as there is evidence in the forests to show. The badger, like the fox, can extend his territory by going right into the hills and settling at high altitudes above Coquetdale and about The Cheviot. Frequently the two are near neighbours. Lower haunts favoured by the badger are the tree and bracken-girt gills and the smaller river valleys from Bewcastle district onward. A recently occupied sett in the banks of the Liddel is within view of one of the forest watch towers.

The often regarded natural trio of fox, badger and otter is truly complete. The otter is plentifully attracted by the many waters among which it has a marked seasonal range. During the warmer months of the year it follows the hill burns and the small lakes and its depredations then among the waterfowl may be as great or greater than those of the fox. It is in the habit of travelling considerable distances overland and in winter it descends to the broader rivers, the Tyne and others, there likely enough to concentrate more on the pursuit of fish.

The Tyne, the northern branch especially, had a record as a salmon and sea trout river particularly outstanding in the days before there was the excessive pollution where it nears the sea; but it is rare, nowadays, for a salmon to ascend as far as the Forest Park. At the western side, these fish run up the feeders of the Esk, the Liddel and the Teviot often to ascend the tributaries as far as water will carry them. All the rivers, including the small hill burns, hold brown trout more or less varying in size, colour and markings according to habitat. Reptiles in the forest lands are represented by the adder or viper, which occurs widely on the moors, and by the common lizard and the slow-worm which are both apparently somewhat more local in their distribution.

Birds are everywhere present as residents, summer visitors or winter visitors, and are distributed according to their choice of habitat. Beginning with a peculiarly British native, the red grouse, the high heather ground supports a strong population, some of the moors having considerable sporting fame. Memories of a brilliant October day include a surprising number of 'reds' seen along the tops between Scotch Knowe and Glendhu. Black grouse, belonging more to the 'white' or grassy ground and the natural growths of birch, alder and rowan, appear to be increasing a little since the time of the great decline affecting the whole country. The far-reaching, bubbling cry of the black-cock is a distinctive spring voice in the land when the males gather at the 'leks' to display before the females, or greyhens. Blackgame habitually come down to the cultivated land but, on a white winter day in Ridsdale, two birds excusably taken to be black grouse, seen perched in a roadside hawthorn, turned out to be red grouse engaged in picking the remaining haws from the branches. Pheasants, long protected on the few big estates near the Forest Park, have recently made their homes in the cover provided by some of the new coniferous plantations; while partridges and woodcock figure occasionally in the old gamebook of Kielder Castle.

The meadow-pipit, the commonest nesting small bird of the moorlands, is the most usual foster-parent of the cuckoos reared among the hills. Its relative, the skylark, goes right to the hill tops, soaring in song above them, while the more typical twite, or mountain linnet, nests sparingly and occasionally on the high ground. The first of the spring arrivals are the wheatear, whose white flash flickers among the rocks and screes, and the ring ouzel, the mountain blackbird, whose sweet piping enlivens faraway gills and cleughs. They may be joined later by an occasional hill-going whinchat; still later, the nightjar arrives on the fringes of bracken and heather. These birds are replaced in winter by the snow buntings which come to feed on the seeds of the moorland rushes, dappling the hillsides with their motley plumage as they fly from one patch to another. Down among the older deciduous trees of the valleys and glens there is that engaging and increasing summer visitor, the pied flycatcher and, along with the more familiar resident tits, the almost twin-like marsh tit and willow tit. In winter, siskins accompany lesser redpolls in the waterside alders, and parties of crossbills appear erratically in the older pines and larches, some of them occasionally staying to breed.

The small birds of the rivers and burns are most typically headed by the dipper, an all-the-year-round songster, now bobbing curtsies from a torrent-washed boulder, next whirring up or down stream; keeping strictly to the winding course of the burn, it is the complete water sprite. The grey wagtail shares its haunts up to the tumbling burns, where they both are most at home, and the pied-wagtail, in its more general distribution, may range as far. Mid-April brings the common sandpiper to grace the watersides and swell the strong company of wading birds.

The grandest of the waders, the curlew, returns in February or March. When its full rippling call rings out over rushy pasture and heather moor there is the true music in this land. This bird, with its peculiar curved bill, has been adopted as the emblem of the Northumberland National Park. The south-westerly passage of departing curlew families is a marked autumn feature of local bird life. Early, as well, the golden plover comes back to nest on hill top or mossy bog; a handsome figure whose liquid note is a real breath of the wild. The dunlin, the 'plover's page', follows on to nest, more sparingly, in places high and low, from Cheviot shoulder to Spadeadam bog. Common snipe are often enough flushed from lough margin or may be heard humming over a hill crest, and woodcock are equally at home in woodlands and on bracken slopes. Down on the haughs and commons the lapwing is a familiar bird, while the redshank not only comes to nest but may also go to the moorlands. More recently too, the oystercatcher has become an inland nester. From the coast it has followed up the rivers and their tributaries, even to the Lewis Burn and the headwaters of the Lyne, so that it is now possible to find 'sea piets' in the shadow of the hills.

This last is not the only bird of the sea to come inland to the Border country. Lesser black-backed gulls have had their moorland colonies, if at present limited to scattered nesters, while odd pairs of the majestic greater black-backed gull have bred on more than one of the flows or peat mosses, and could do so again. The black-headed gull, more thoroughly an inland nester, has colonies which wax and wane or shift from one lough to another. A good year has seen eight hundred pairs at Linsheels Lough, and fifty at Grindon, but an off-season a mere handful, just as the birds come and go.

The nearest large heronry, with some ten nests, is at Chillingham. Smaller ones can be found about Wark and in Redesdale, although single nests in scattered haunts are becoming more and more frequent. Anyway, the birds that resort to the tall trees in these places forage widely and, often enough, a lone heron may be found wading some distant burn or heavily winging over a hill top from one valley to another.

The changing conditions, as they affect birds, have encouraged a remarkable rise in the numbers of short-eared owls. Previous to the planting of the moorlands there were no more than scattered pairs which could be anywhere between Upper Coquetdale and the wastes of Bewcastle. There were of course those exceptional times, now a matter of history, when plagues of field voles, their staple prey, were responsible for a temporarily large population in the Borderland. With the present attractions of food and habitat these ground-nesting owls are clearly becoming increasingly plentiful, the many established pairs preferring the expanses where the trees are still small and shifting their home quarters accordingly. The long-eared owl, a sparse resident having a fondness for conifers, now at any rate has a wider choice; the tawny owl can be found in old buildings as well as old woodlands, and the barn owl keeps to the outlying farmsteads, or maybe some crannied outcrop of rock.

Several notable birds of prey occasionally call in as visitors. A golden eagle which lingered during a recent April month had its nightly roost on Christianbury Crags. One of our native buzzards was lately at Kershope and the rough-legged buzzard from overseas has a record of winter occurrences. Two kinds of harriers—Montagu's and the Hen Harrier, are known to have nested in this region in 1960, though both are very scarce. The resident sparrow-hawk reaches the last outliers of the trees, and the merlin, so characteristic of the moorland and nesting typically in the heather, has the kestrel for company. Here the kestrel is very much a bird of the cleughs and small rocky scars and, as a note of special interest, now and then nests on the detached mass of rock known as the Kielder Stone. Elsewhere it adopts a disused nest of the carrion crow.

The most peerless of feathered hunters, the peregrine falcon, has a number of breeding sites from which its forays extend all over the forests. Besides its regularly-used eyries on The Cheviot and in the Simonside Hills, there are others likely to be occupied every now and again in Coquetdale, Redesdale and Kielder. Whether a resident or a roaming caller, a speeding peregrine is one of the finest sights in wild life the forests afford.

The whole of the forests is the land of the raven, from the Cheviot to the edge of Spadeadam, and from Harwood to the bounds of Newcastleton or, as it is still called by its own folk, Copshaw Holme. It is hereabouts that an aged alder and a tree in a stand of magnificent old Scots pines have supported nests during these last few years when the raven has apparently increased and reverted to nesting more in trees. Crag nesting sites, however, remain much the more favoured and Kielder has the distinction of having perhaps the

63

most remote in all England, one which is seven long moorland miles from a highway. A simple rocky outcrop, it is so coated with the tell-tale green 'stain' that it must have been used for many generations, if not centuries.

Our own times have seen this Borderland become a meeting place of birds which have extended their breeding range either from the north or from the south. The green woodpecker, in its rather amazing spread, has come up to vie with the already established great spotted woodpecker and ranges from Harwood to Liddesdale, including the plantations of Redesdale; the lesser spotted, or barred woodpecker, has also been seen. Previously the goosander had come down to settle on the burns of Coquetdale and Newcastleton, while still earlier the wigeon colonised the lochs and loughs. These lakes attract a fascinating array of waterfowl, season by season. Besides the constant mallard, pairs of which stray far up the hill burns, there are teal and maybe shoveller, tufted duck, pochard and little grebe among the nesters. Waterhen and coot are regulars and pintail and great crested grebe have been known to breed. Winter brings goosanders in plenty, goldeneye and an abundance of tufted duck and pochard, and then there are wild swans and geese. Whooper swans come regularly and in numbers and Bewick's swans now and again. The goose visitors, at one time bean geese in quantity, are nowadays other grey species in small gaggles, either grey lag, white-fronted or, as is most likely, pink-footed geese. All contribute to form some noble gatherings of fowl.

The effect on bird life of current developments can be illustrated by reference to a few of our best-known birds. With more trees, woodpigeons now outnumber the stock-doves which years ago arrived to nest in old, hollow trunks and in the crannies of rocks. The dainty little willow warbler sings as sweetly from the new growth as from the last birch tree up a valley, and the jaunty wren pours out the more lusty song of a hardy mite that roams still farther to the hidden recesses of the hills. Parts of the forests are now old enough to have attracted the goldcrests in nesting time and unmistakable low trillings constantly betoken their presence. (With this tiny one and the whooper swan the forests claim both the smallest and the biggest of true British birds). The friendly notes of such familiar songsters as the chaffinch, song thrush and dunnock are ever to be heard ringing out from the shelter of the young conifers.

Rarer visitors recorded by Head Forester W. L. McCavish, a keen bird watcher, include waxwings, a grey-backed shrike, a diver, a golden oriole and also an occasional snow bunting.

As often as not, a naturalist has the benefit of companionship in the field, the stimulus of talk with a kindred spirit and the advantage

SKETCH MAP OF THE BORDER FORESTS

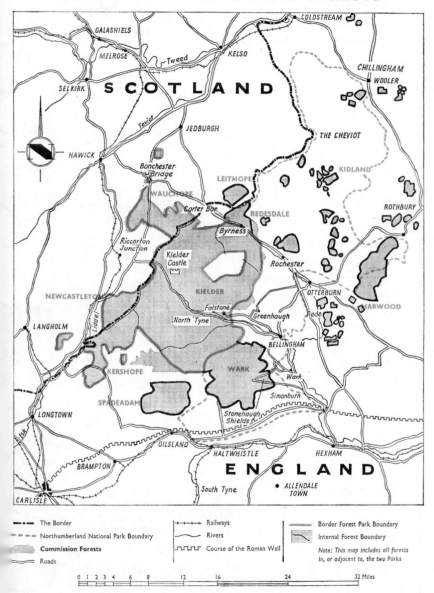

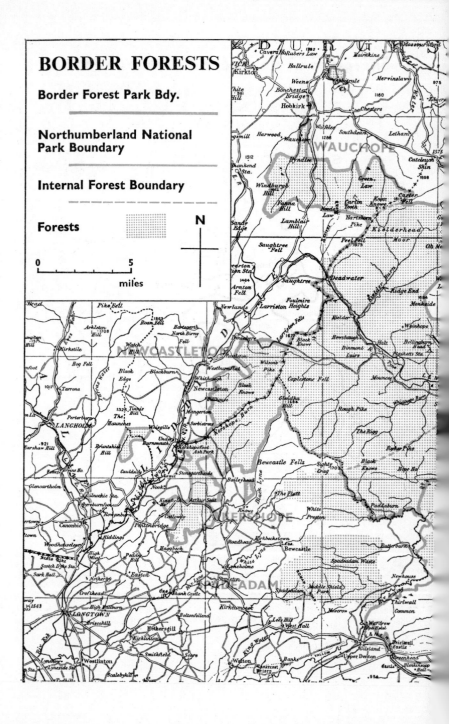

BORDER FORESTS

Border Forest Park Bdy.

Northumberland National Park Boundary

Internal Forest Boundary

Forests

N

0   5

miles

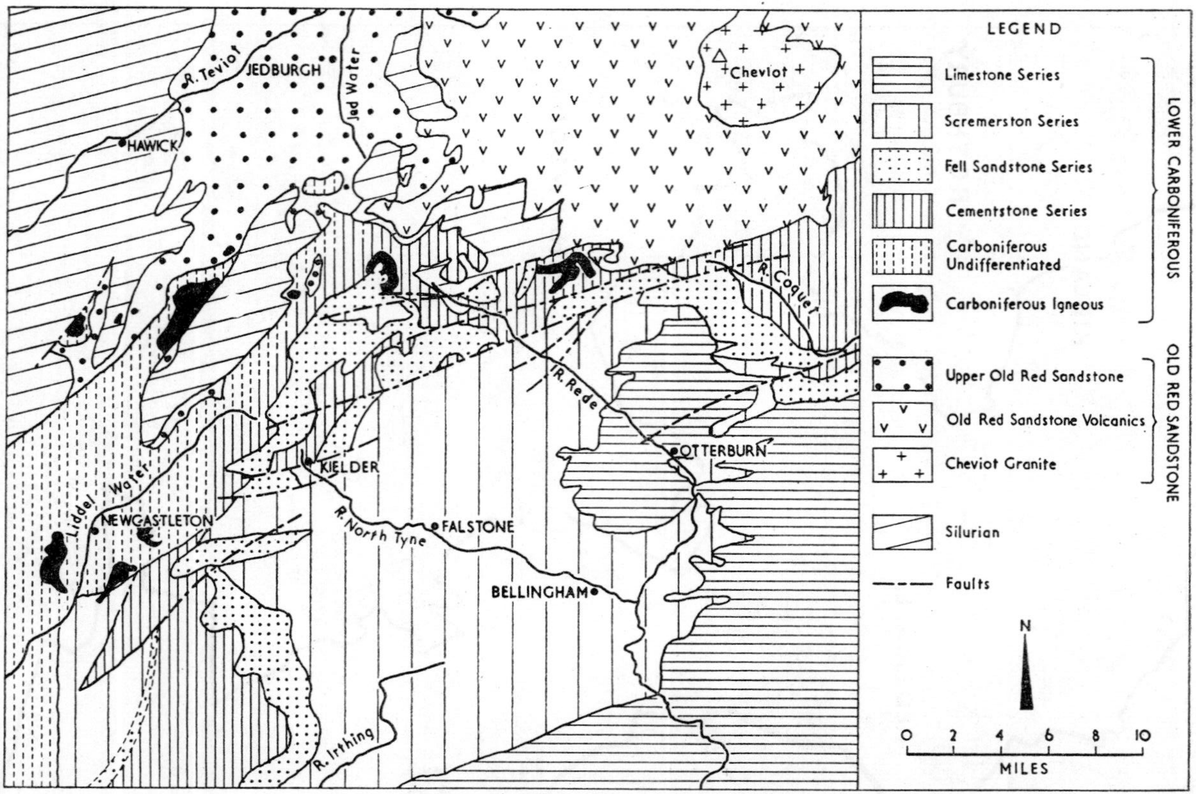

Geological Map of the Border Region

LEGEND

LOWER CARBONIFEROUS

Limestone Series
Scremerston Series
Fell Sandstone Series
Cementstone Series
Carboniferous Undifferentiated
Carboniferous Igneous

OLD RED SANDSTONE

Upper Old Red Sandstone
Old Red Sandstone Volcanics
Cheviot Granite

Silurian

Faults

N

0 2 4 6 8 10
MILES

Cheviot

R. Coquet

OTTERBURN

R. Rede

Jed Water

JEDBURGH

R. Teviot

HAWICK

KIELDER

FALSTONE

R. North Tyne

BELLINGHAM

R. Irthing

Liddel Water

NEWCASTLETON

of the printed word. My acknowledgments are due to **Dr. Derek Ratcliffe** of Carlisle and **Mr. Matthew Phillipson** of Haltwhistle.

BORDER NAMES FOR BEASTS AND BIRDS

Brock ... ... =	Badger (Gaelic, *brochg*)
Corbie ... ... =	Crow (French, *corbeau*)
Esk ... ... =	Snake (Gaelic, *easg*, eel)
Foumart ... ... =	Polecat (foul (smelling) *marten*)
Gimmer ... ... =	Young ewe (Norse, *gimmerlam*)
Hoolet ... ... =	Owl (Norse, *ugle*)
Hurcheon (Urchin) ... =	Hedgehog (French, *hérisson*)
Mavis ... ... =	Thrush (French, *mauvis*)
Mawkin ... ... =	Hare
Merle ... ... =	Blackbird (French, *merle*)
Moldiwarp or Moldie =	(Norse, *moldvarp*)
Rae ... ... =	Roe deer (Norse, *raa*)
Sweetmart ... ... =	Pine marten (sweet marten)
Tod ... ... =	Fox
Yorlin ... ... =	Yellowhammer (Welsh, *aur Ilinos*, golden linnet)
Yowe ... ... =	Ewe

The survival of old Celtic, Norse and Norman French names is remarkable.

The Kielder Stone

Ah Tam! Gie me a Border burn
That canna rin without a turn,
And wi its bonnie babble fills
The glens amang oor native hills
          —J. B. Selkirk

GEOLOGY

BY DR. G. A. L. JOHNSON

Geology is one of the basic factors on which the natural flora of the Forest Park and its capacity to produce timber depend. Both the general topography of the area and the form and disposition of its soils are directly related to the solid geology of the region. The soils of the area are complex and will be mentioned later in the chapter but the topographical relation is more straightforward. In the north the presence of more resistant strata gives rise to the rounded Border Hills, the westward continuation of the Cheviots, while to the south the rather less resistant rocks form the undulating moorland of Cumberland and Northumberland. The area is nowhere of great height, but reaches almost 2,000 feet at Peel Fell, the highest point in the district. The general distribution of the rocks is shown in the geological map facing page 65.

The geological history of the area may be divided into two spans of greatly differing length and separated by a long interval of time. Firstly the solid rocks were formed mainly on the floor of an ancient sea and in shallow estuaries, but partly in shallow lakes and on a land surface. They are assigned to the Silurian, Devonian and Carboniferous eras, and consist of a great thickness of sediments of all grades, varying from coarse conglomerates to grits, sandstones, fine shales and limestones, the sorted accumulations of rock debris derived from some ancient highland long since disappeared. During this long period of time, for over 70 million years passed while these rocks were being formed, volcanoes erupted in this area at two different periods and left evidence of their prolonged activity in vast quantities of lava and ash preserved among the sediments. This chapter of geological history ended some 240 million years ago and there followed a long interval which left no trace of its passing on the present countryside. Then during Tertiary times, a few tens of millions of years ago, the geological processes started which formed the topography we see today. This period is essentially one of erosion of the solid rocks and formation of superficial deposits; the peat and soil which now cover the area slowly accumulated during the latter part of this time.

The thickness of the sequence of sedimentary rocks, including the intercalated igneous lava and ash, is of the order of eight thousand feet or more, but owing to the gentle inclination or dip of the strata the whole thickness is visible within this area. The dip of the beds is in a general south-easterly direction so that the oldest rocks are in the north and towards the south they get progressively younger. The area actually lies within a broad shallow syncline between the Cheviot mass on the north-east and the Bewcastle anticline on the south-west. The structure of the area is complicated by faulting which considerably dislocates the simple succession of strata.

GEOLOGICAL SEQUENCE

SUPERFICIAL DEPOSITS   *Approximate thickness*

Recent:
   Hill Peat and Basin Peat   .   .   .   .   .   —
   Alluvium   .   .   .   .   —

Pleistocene:
   Glacial ground-moraine   .   .   .   .   .   .   Up to 120 feet

SOLID FORMATIONS

Carboniferous:
   Carboniferous Limestone Series:
      Alternation of limestones, shales and sandstones
      with thin coal seams forming a Yoredale sequence   Over 2,000 feet
   Scremerston Series:
      Shale and sandstone succession with thin lime-
      stone bands and many small coal seams   .   .   2,500 feet
   Fell Sandstone Series:
      Massive sandstones and grits separated by shales   600 feet
   Cementstone Series:
      Shales, muddy limestones and sandstones   .   .   700 feet

Devonian:
  Upper Old Red Sandstone:
    Red and mottled sandstones and marls . . At least 300 feet
  Lower Old Red Sandstone:
    Lava and agglomerate with sandstone and marl . Several thousand feet
Silurian:
  Wenlock Series:
    Shales and graywackes . . . . . Unknown thickness

PRE-CARBONIFEROUS SEDIMENTS

The oldest rocks of the district are the grey shales and graywackes of Wenlock, Silurian age. These beds lie mainly on the northern side of the Border and underlie much of the Forest Park about Wauchope. They consist of grey and greenish-grey shales separated by bands of medium and coarse-grained graywacke, a strongly cemented dark coloured sandstone. The rocks are mainly unfossiliferous but occasional bands in the shale contain poorly preserved graptolites indicative of marine deposition. The beds have been much faulted and folded and high dips are general.

The Lower Old Red Sandstone which overlies the Wenlock beds is only represented in this area by small patches of red sandstone, marl and conglomerate associated with the lavas which dominate this sequence. The Upper Old Red Sandstone is better developed and overlies the Silurian and Lower Old Red Sandstone with marked unconformity; a long period of erosion is probable between the deposition of the Lower and Upper Old Red Sandstone. The beds of the Upper Old Red Sandstone are composed of bright red and mottled sandstones and marls containing infrequent but well preserved fossil fish. The succession was laid down in wide shallow lakes surrounded by desert conditions and is several hundred feet thick; it outcrops within the Forest Park at several places about the Border.

CARBONIFEROUS SEDIMENTS

The Upper Old Red Sandstone is succeeded by Carboniferous sediments with complete conformity, but the conditions of deposition underwent a marked change. Shallow lakes and desert gradually gave way to shallow marine and estuarine conditions, and during Lower Carboniferous times in this area marine deposition became increasingly more important. The uppermost Old Red Sandstone beds are continued at the base of the Carboniferous as a series of flaggy sandstones and clays within the Cementstone Series. The Cementstone Series proper consists of a thick succession of light coloured shales, shaly-limestones and subordinate sandstones. The

Series is relatively unfossiliferous but marine fossils and fossil plant debris are present; towards the top the thicker limestones contain abundant calcareous algae. The succession is of shallow water estuarine origin. Along the Border the low undulating ground is formed by the Cementstones which have a wide outcrop across the area below the Fell Sandstone moors. The Series is well exposed in Deadwater Burn.

Above the Cementstones the Fell Sandstones are typically coarse massive false-bedded sandstones intercalated with marls, lilac and grey shales and rare coal seams. The sandstones are often close together and thick so that they form well developed scars in series on the high fells, and from them the sequence takes its name. The Series outcrops in a broad semicircle mostly to the south of the Border between Kershope and Carter Fell and forms the highest ground in the area. There are no sharp boundaries to the Fell Sandstones; below they grade into the Cementstones and above into the Scremerston Series. They are relatively unfossiliferous but what fossils there are, together with the presence of thin coal seams, indicate deposition in shallow water estuarine conditions and indeed some of the beds may even be of aeolian, that is, wind-borne, origin.

The Scremerston Series consists of a succession of some 2,500 feet of limestones, sandy-limestones, sandstones, shales and many thin coal seams. The Series resembles the Cementstones proper in some respects, but differs in the presence of many coal seams and numerous marine fossils at certain horizons. This Series is well exposed in Lewis Burn and Plashetts Burn. The principal marine horizons are the limestones, most of which are impure and grade towards calcareous flagstones. Sandstones and shales are important members of the succession; the former tend to be very variable and massive sandstones are uncommon. Workable coal seams are present and have been extensively mined at some places, notably at Plashetts. The seams tend to vary rapidly in thickness and character over quite short distances and are very numerous, often as many as one to every 30 or 40 feet of strata; but they are usually thin, an average being about 8 inches.

The Carboniferous Limestone Series lies above the Scremerston beds and forms a well-defined unit characterised by the rhythmic deposition of the stratal sequence; limestone, shale, sandstone, coal being repeated many times over to form a Yoredale sequence. The thick marine limestones and shales developed in the lower part of this Series demonstrate the continued increase in importance of marine conditions of deposition. The area of outcrop lies to the south and east of the Forest Park.

The igneous rocks of the area consist of extrusive lavas, agglomerates, intrusive dykes and sills, with the major Cheviot granite intrusion to the north-east; they belong to three separate periods of time. The oldest igneous rocks are the great mass of igneous lavas and agglomerate of Lower Old Red Sandstone age which outcrop over a wide area to the north and east. This volcanic episode was terrestial and commenced with an explosive phase producing vast quantities of ash and agglomerate. It was followed by rhyolite and andesite lavas which finally formed a total of several thousands of feet of volcanic deposits. Surrounded by the lavas at the eastern side of this outcrop, the intrusive Cheviot granite, a typical red granite, forms the high ground of Cheviot and Hedgehope Hill. It was intruded shortly after the volcanic episode, for boulders of the granite are incorporated in the basement Carboniferous conglomerates. Many porphyrite and felsite dykes, which cut both lavas and granite, represent the last stage of this period of igneous activity.

The second period of volcanicity took place during early Carboniferous times. Again large quantities of lava and ash were produced from many centres on the northern side of the Border. The extrusive rocks consist of basalt lava-flows, with ashes and agglomerate sometimes infilling ancient volcanic necks. Volcanic centres of this type occur at Wauchope and Windburgh Hill. A later stage of the Carboniferous volcanicity was the intrusion of many dolerite dykes and sills. The dykes have a general E.N.E.-W.S.W. trend; examples can be seen in Deadwater Burn and Lewis Burn. Intrusive dolerite sills of similar age occur at Carter Fell, Lumsdon Law and elsewhere in the area.

The final phase of the igneous activity took place in Tertiary times and is represented by dykes having a west-north-west trend. The rocks themselves have a marked petrological resemblance to the numerous Tertiary dykes which converge on Mull. These can be traced at intervals across Scotland towards the local dykes whose age is thus fairly certain. The dyke at Kielder Head and others near Kielder Castle are of this age.

GLACIAL DEPOSITS

The whole of Britain north of a line joining the estuaries of the Thames and Severn was covered by continental ice-sheets during the last Ice Age; a glacial episode which ended only some 25,000 years ago. In Northern England deposits of glacial origin are widespread but clear exposures are relatively rare, thus the division of the drift deposits into different members and the tracing of the various members is difficult. In the Forest Park district the glacial drift consists normally of a tough, grey-blue and brown Boulder Clay. To the north and west of the North Tyne this deposit covers wide stretches of country up to a height of 1,400 feet in places. On the east the deposits are not so extensive, a fact which is in accordance with the general rule and indicates that the drift came from the north and west. This is confirmed by the foreign erratic boulders present in the Boulder Clay, which consist of Galloway granites and Silurian graywacke and shale, with other rocks derived from the north-west. Yet a further indication of the direction of ice movement is afforded by the presence of glacial striations with a general south-easterly trend on smooth surfaces of rock. Locally, where quantities of rock debris from a certain stratum are incorporated in a Boulder Clay, it may become strikingly different in character; thus reddened Boulder Clays are found where much of the Fell Sandstone shales have been incorporated.

An upper Boulder Clay, composed mainly of sandstone blocks in a brown-yellow clay, has been recorded as resting on the normal tough grey Boulder Clay. This upper drift is thought to represent a deposit formed by solifluxion (soil creep) during early post-glacial times when periglacial (permanently frozen subsoil) conditions prevailed in the area. Solifluxion deposits are widespread on high ground in Northern England and are often characterised by the presence of many sandstone boulders, some of which tend to be upended in the surface of the deposit. The occurrence of drifts of this type below deep peat can be seen on Bewshaugh Moor and in many other places; the widespread nature of this deposit, here as elsewhere, indicates a prolonged period of frozen ground conditions at the end of the last glaciation.

Although three phases have been described in the glaciation of Northern England, characterised by boulder clays of differing composition, no satisfactory interglacial deposits have been found. The phases were long regarded as being separate glaciations equivalent to those of the Continent of Europe. Recently, however, the evidence has been re-examined and the glacial deposits are now regarded *by some* as being formed by a single complex glaciation— the inference being that only the most extensive of the Continental glaciations covered Northern England. Certainly there is little evidence that the local Boulder Clay has its origins in anything but a single glaciation and this was followed by a considerable period of frozen ground conditions.

RECENT DEPOSITS

Old river terraces of gravel are present at several places in the

71

North Tyne valley, particularly at the foot of Lewis Burn close to the camp site. Elsewhere, valley bottom alluvium is fairly widespread and is well developed about Deadwater and Falstone. The smaller streams have a rapid fall and their flats are composed mainly of sands and gravel.

Peat deposits form a general covering to the fells and occasionally completely fill well-defined basins. The blanket peat is often under 18 inches thick but in places reaches six feet or more. Where thick peat deposits are found with the basal layers visible, a band packed with the stumps and roots of birch is often found near the bottom of the peat, often almost resting on a solifluxion deposit. At least one other wood layer has been recorded at a higher horizon in the peat. The thick peat deposits are prone to rapid erosion should conditions about them change even slightly; abundant evidence of past and present peat erosion is to be seen in the area. The widespread thin blanket peat frequently has no well defined basal wood layer and is often the residue of earlier eroded peat deposits recolonised by vegetation; isolated hummocks of peat are in some areas the only evidence of previous blanket peat cover.

The basin peat deposits infill hollows, perhaps in part of glacial origin, and may exceed 20 feet in thickness. Two of these basin deposits, Falstone Moss and Broadgate Fell, have been studied in detail by Dr. Kathleen Blackburn (1953) who finds evidence to suggest the possibility of two periods in which the bogs were sufficiently dry to support trees. There are records of the use of bog timber in the Kielder district and the deeper peats are still being cut for fuel in some places.

SOILS

The Forest Park area embraces a considerable variation in soil types many of which are derived from the Boulder Clay and other drift deposits. Straight soils derived directly from the underlying solid formations are rare. In the north of the area the Silurian shales weather to a rusty or ochreous yellow clay and produce heavy yellow loams which contain varying amounts of drift material. The Carboniferous shales similarly produce heavy grey loams but are almost everywhere covered by glacial drifts. The thicker limestones occasionally crop out at the surface in broad bands and on weathering produce a fertile red-brown heavy loam. Other heavy loams are produced on the local Boulder Clay, especially where it is mainly derived from Carboniferous shales. Light and loamy sands are found on outcrops of sandstone and the widespread sandy solifluxion deposit gives rise to more loamy soils of this type, as do the spreads of alluvium.

Looking up the North Tyne Valley near Emmethaugh, Kielder Forest

The Trek to the Camp Site

Stannersburn Village in North Tynedale

Stonehaugh Village, Wark Forest

Drainage of the land is poor over the fell tops so that soils of the gley group are widespread and on them the peat deposits are formed. On the better drained slopes peaty podsols and brown earth type soils are to be found; the latter are perhaps partly due to the presence of natural woodlands which existed over large areas up to relatively recent times.

EVOLUTION OF THE PRESENT LANDSCAPE

The sculpture of the present landscape began in Tertiary times with the gradual sub-aerial denudation of the area and excavation of the valleys out of the gently inclined country rocks. This inclination directed the formation of the consequent streams, now the rivers North Tyne and Rede. As time progressed the comparative resistance of the sedimentary formations to erosion caused valleys to form in the softer beds and directed the course of the subsequent streams such as Kielder Burn and Lewis Burn. At the same time the more resistant formations became elevated with respect to the softer and more easily eroded surrounding rocks and gave the high ground we know today in the Fell Sandstone scarps and Border hills.

The formation of the landscape had proceeded a long way by the beginning of the Pleistocene Ice Age, but this episode left a widespread and lasting impression on the area. As the deterioration of climate proceeded at the beginning of the glacial period, permanent ice-caps formed on the hills to the north. Later a great ice-sheet, forced from the west and north over the district, covered the lower hills up to at least 1,700 feet, thinning and spreading out towards the east. The scouring action of this ice-sheet is evident in the rounded hills, striated pavements and great quantities of Boulder Clay formed from the planed-off materials.

When the climate moderated, the ice dwindled and streams began to re-excavate valleys now choked with glacial deposits. Many of the streams ran along their old valley courses but elsewhere rocky gorges were formed. The area was gradually recolonised with vegetation; traces of these early floras being now preserved at the base of some of the peat basins.

In post-glacial times erosion by streams continued with the deposition of alluvium on the valley floors. Some of this takes the form of shingle and gravel which have proved useful for the building of forest roads. Much of the area, however, is still covered with fairly homogeneous Boulder Clay, giving the comparatively featureless rounded hills of the Cementstone and Scremerston outcrops. The higher ground is relatively free of glacial drift, for where present the deposits tend to be eroded rapidly; thus the Fell Sandstone heights have well-exposed sandstone scars. Slight climatic changes during this period allowed forests to form, later to be covered by peat, and trees to colonise part of the area again. The recent destruction of the woodland in the area is in part attributed to man through widespread sheep-grazing on the fells.

Bibliography

The geology of the area is shown on the following maps published by the Geological Survey of Great Britain:

England:
  1-inch to the mile, sheet 7 (Kielder Castle) and 8 (Elsdon), New Series.
  1-inch to the mile, sheet 12 (Newcastle) and 13 (Bellingham), Old Series only.
Scotland:
  1-inch to one mile, sheet 11 (Langholm) and 17 (Jedburgh).

The Geological Survey Memoirs covering this area are:

CLOUGH, C. T. 1889. *The Geology of Plashetts and Kielder.* (Explanation of Sheet 7). H.M.S.O., London.

MILLER, H. 1887. *The Geology of Otterburn and Elsdon.* (Explanation of Sheet 8). H.M.S.O., London.

Other publications dealing with the area include:

EASTWOOD, T. 1946. *British Regional Geology: Northern England.* (2nd Edition). H.M.S.O., London, which gives selected references on pages 67-68.

We tracked the green Catrail
Winding like a snake,
Where bluebells lisp and flutter
And solemn thistles quake,
For fear the buried hill-men
Should hear them and awake.

Penchrise—Marion Angus

WALKING IN THE BORDERS

BY H. L. EDLIN

The Border Forest Park and its surroundings provide some of the grandest walks in the country, but until the formation of the camping ground at Lewisburn, and the opening of the Kielder Youth Hostel, much of it was inaccessible by reason of its distance from centres of accommodation and means of transport; hence it remained little known. Although there are no very high hills, there are plenty of remote ones, and the stoutest of walkers can find ample scope to exercise his powers of endurance and knowledge of way-finding and map reading. The following selection of routes has been made on a geographical basis to serve several centres. It includes some that are little more than pleasant strolls, others which, though long, are straightforward with good footing, and a few over the peaty hilltops along the Border Line or the Christianbury Crags which will only appeal to those ready to slog in stout boots over boggy ground, with few landmarks to guide them. So the character of each has been set down, and should be noted before a choice is made.

Because the Forest Park is not a static, but a developing landscape, maps soon get out of date. New plantations are made, new roads developed, and however carefully a map is drawn it can only show the state of affairs at the date of printing; so discretion is needed for interpreting even recent maps of the Park.

Because of the limitations of scale on this guide's map (three miles to one inch at best) anyone who embarks on the longer hill walks is advised to equip himself with the appropriate Ordnance Survey Sheet or Sheets on the one-inch scale (details on page 100). All the new forest roads are open to the walker, and as most are untarred and carry only occasional traffic they provide pleasant going.

The big distances between the dales should never be overlooked. It is scarcely ever possible to go over from one dale to the next and return the same day on foot. So arrangements for a return by public transport, or an overnight stay, are often needed. A round tour of all the forests, entirely on foot, could well occupy four days. Starting at Haltwhistle, Wark Forest could be crossed to Bellingham the first day; Byrness in Redesdale Forest could be reached on the second; on the third one could go over to the Lewisburn camp site or the Kielder Youth Hostel in North Tynedale, and on the fourth, cross to the Kershope Burn to end up at Newcastleton or Kershopefoot in Liddesdale.

Two areas should be avoided; neither lies within the Park but the visitor might be tempted to use them as approaches. One is the vast Spadeadam Waste north of Gilsland, on the headwaters of the River Irthing; much of this is reserved for defence works, the rest is trackless and marshy, with distances too great to be traversed with safety. The other region lies due north of Rochester on the east of Redesdale Forest, and forms a military firing range.

Within the Park itself there are no such distractions, and the thoughtful visitor who respects the Country Code will be welcome along every track and path. But do please remember that this is both a farming district where a gate mistakenly left open or shut can cause the shepherds much unnecessary worry, and also a forested countryside where fire precautions are the constant pre-occupation of the foresters.

A number of the walks have been marked with coloured indicators, and where this is so the colour is stated in the accounts that follow. In some cases these colour-marked routes run right across the Park, and since the distances are then too great for all but the hardiest of hikers, only a portion of each is included in each walk.

A few words of warning—if, despite these directions—you wander off the track, remember the old dodge of following water downhill until you reach civilisation. It may mean a surprisingly long hike from some points in the Park, but it will always bring you to safety somewhere. Again—should you blunder into the trees, remember that they are planted in straight—or at least continuous lines; follow any line steadily and you will soon come out on a road or open grassy track.

Do not, unless you know the ground well, go off on a lone hike. Even if you go in a party, make sure that somebody is told of your proposed route before you set out; otherwise the task of a search party in these vast hills would be a hopeless one.

WALKS BETWEEN LIDDESDALE AND NORTH TYNEDALE
(Kershope, Newcastleton and Kielder Forests)
(See also Nos. 18 and 19.)

1. *Kershopefoot to Scots Knowe, by Forest Roads.*
9 miles (Ordnance Survey Sheet 76).   Yellow signs.

From Kershopefoot Station take the county road eastwards for half a mile, and turn left at the road junction. Two hundred yards farther on, just before reaching the bridge over the Kershope Burn, take the forest road on the right. This runs for 1½ miles up the lovely Kershope Valley, crosses a county road near a second bridge over the Kershope Burn (where it is said that excisemen once hid to catch smugglers taking salt into England) and then follows the river for a further mile. Then it bears left and crosses the Kershope Burn into Scotland by a concrete bridge; it continues close to this burn, up its north side, for a further four miles. After the road ends, proceed for another 200 yards along the track to the Scots Knowe.

This point is famous as the meeting place of three counties, the Scottish Roxburghshire and the English Cumberland and Northumberland. A march fence between the two latter counties makes it easy to find. The counties actually meet at the junction of two burns, 1,041 feet above sea level; the Knowe, now clad in trees, is on the Scottish side.

2. *Scots Knowe to Newcastleton, by Forest Roads*
9 miles (O.S. Sheet 76).   Blue signs.

The return journey can be made by following the outward route for 2½ miles to the point where a road strikes off right. This winds uphill for 2½ miles to the cottages and fields of Tweedenhead. Thence the route runs to the right hand side of the Tweeden Burn, and climbs slowly for two miles to the forest edge. At the point marked "Chairman's View" a wonderful prospect of Liddesdale opens out, and away to the south you can glimpse the Solway Firth. The road emerges near Dykecrofts; turn left and descend through fields for two miles to Newcastleton.

3. *Scots Knowe to Bloody Bush. Hill Walk, 2 miles.*
(O.S. Sheet 76.)   Fence line.

Although there is no made path, it is a simple matter for a sturdy walker to continue the ascent of the Kershope Burn, here called

'Clark's Sike', to Hobb's Flow. A fence line follows the Border acros this bog, which can be crossed in dry weather, or skirted if the ground is too damp. The fence runs straight to the Bloody Bush boundary mark, a stone obelisk some twenty feet high, on the old road. The return to Liddesdale can be made by turning left and following this road, described under **4** below. There are no signs on this route, as the fence line is easy to follow.

3a. (Note: It is proposed to develop a forest road from Scots Knowe to join the Bloody Bush route farther east, near Willow Bog, and when this is done it will provide an easier route; a cleared track already exists.)

4. *Steele Road to Bloody Bush* (5 *miles*) *and the Lewisburn Camp Site* (12 *miles*) *by the old Toll Road into Tynedale.*
(O.S. Sheet 76.) Road.
From Steele Road station descend eastwards to the Newcastleton-Jedburgh road, at a point 4 miles north of Newcastleton. Turn right and then left, and you are on the old track into the North Tyne valley, which provides a fine route for the walker, though it is not passable for cars. It ascends to 1,500 feet on the Larriston Fells, then drops to 1,312 feet at the Bloody Bush, scene of an ancient affray, where the Border is crossed. From then on it is a straightforward descent down through the spruce woods of Kielder Forest, following first the Akenshaw Burn and then the Lewis Burn. About 1½ miles below Bloody Bush, one reaches an old plantation called Buck Fell, close to the farmstead of Willow Bog. Here, route **3a** from the Scots Knowe (mentioned above) strikes in from the right, and for a stretch the road carries yellow signs.

Continuing down the dale, the public road through the North Tyne valley is struck just opposite the camp site; a left turn here leads to the Kielder Youth Hostel, two miles up the dale.

4a. To reach Kielder Castle and the Youth Hostel by a more direct route, leave the road just past Akenshawburn, which is the second farmstead down the dale. Just after you have crossed a stone bridge, turn left up a forest road for 500 yards; where this road bends right, go straight on uphill, and descend north-west; this path is three miles long, and is marked by yellow signs.

5. *Bloody Bush to Bells Linn, along the Border Line. Hill Walk.*
(O.S. Sheet 76) (6 miles). Fence line.
It is a fairly simple matter to follow the actual Border north-east from Bloody Bush, into the Kielder valley; it is clearly marked by a

78

fence line all the way. But the going for the first three miles is rough, boggy, and heavy. The Line runs north-east for one mile to a point 1,610 feet high on the Larriston Fells—the highest point touched between Kershope and Kielder. Then it swings east for 1½ miles, following an ill-defined ridge, to Buckside Knowe, 1,351 feet. Here it turns north, and drops steeply for half a mile, down an un-named stream, to join Bell's Burn beside a pyramidal pillar—one of the few clear landmarks on this stretch of the Border. Thence the route runs down Bell's Burn to Bell's Linn, a deep cleft with small waterfalls and clear pools. A few hundred yards farther on the burn reaches the main North Tyne road, which can be followed south-eastwards towards Kielder Youth Hostel (3 miles) and the Lewisburn Camp site (5 miles).

The actual Border, however, turns north-west from Bell's Linn to ascend Thorlieshope Pike, 1,180 feet. Thence it turns east to the old Deadwater Station, follows the track of the old railway north for a quarter of a mile, and swings east again to cross the road at a point marked by a sign saying 'England'.

WALKS BETWEEN NORTH TYNEDALE AND REDESDALE
(Kielder, Wauchope and Redesdale Forests)

6. *Deadwater to Peel Fell (3 miles) the Kielder Stone (4½ miles) and Knox Knowe (7 miles).*

(O.S. Sheet 70.)   Blue signs.

Peel Fell, 1,975 feet above sea level, is at once the highest and the most accessible of the summits of the Forest Park, and commands the widest views. It is best ascended from Deadwater, by following a forest road that enters the woods on the north side about one mile east of the Scottish Border. After two miles this road swings west, crosses a burn, and ends in a track that runs west to the Border, here marked by a fence and a stone dike. Here bear right and start the steady climb along the *edge* of the sprucewoods; the footing is good almost to the summit, although there is a rise of 700 feet in a distance of one mile. A small area on the top is covered by a deep peat moss, and there are two cairns. That on the Scottish side gives a wide view down Liddesdale to the Solway Firth, thirty miles away. That on the English side, which marks the actual summit, commands a broad expanse of Northumbria, extending, on a clear day, to the North Sea, forty miles distant; for this is one of the few places in Britain from which one may see both east and west coasts. Deadwater, by the way, is three miles north of Kielder Hostel, or five from the camp site.

From the summit, the fence line that marks the course of the border may be followed for one mile north-eastwards down the course of a burn to the famous Kielder Stone, an enormous detached block of sandstone. It is said that this post once served as a Border 'post office', letters being left by messengers of one country for collection by those of the other, in the days when it was unsafe for an emissary to venture into the enemy's territory; the hole below its south corner may have been the 'letter box'. Look at the north corner for the carved initials 'N' and a reversed 'D', standing respectively for the Duke of Northumberland and the Duke of Douglas. These, and the vertical line between them, form the boundary marks of two great estates, one in England and the other in Scotland. Only a skilful climber should try to ascend the stone, as the holds are poor and hard to find on the way down.

6a. From the Kielder Stone the easiest return route (blue signs) is that down the course of the Scalp Burn to Kielder Head, four miles away, and thence by the forest road (yellow signs) down the Kielder Burn to Kielder Castle, four miles further on.

6b. A diversion (white signs) to Knox Knowe is well worth while for the glorious panoramic view it affords over the Jed Forest and Rule Water country on the Scottish side. Descending from the Stone, cross the burn that comes down on the left, climb a short steep slope and keep safely above Wylies Crags, following the old Border fence to the next stream junction, 1 mile ahead. Knox Knowe now lies ahead, 1½ miles away to the north-east, up a steady slope with firm footing.

At this point, 1,636 feet above sea level, an old raiders' route crosses the Border. You may follow it north (**6c**) down the Black Burn through Wauchope Forest, to reach first the small camp site at Burns Cottage, and then the main road from Carter Bar to Hawick close to Southdean, five miles away. From Burns Cottage on, the forest road provides an easier route to the main road than does the footpath shown on maps.

6d. Or you may turn south from Knox Knowe, to follow a route with white signs down the slopes between the Scalp Burn and Grey Mare's Knowe, to Kielder Head, four miles away. Kielder Castle lies a further four miles down the forest road, which is marked with yellow signs. This route, *taken in reverse*, is the easiest way to reach Knox Knowe from Kielder Castle.

6e. *Knox Knowe to Carter Bar. Hill Walk, 6 miles.*
(O.S. Sheet 70.)   No signs.
This route follows the actual Border Line, indicated for most of the way by a fence line or occasional cairns. It follows the watershed

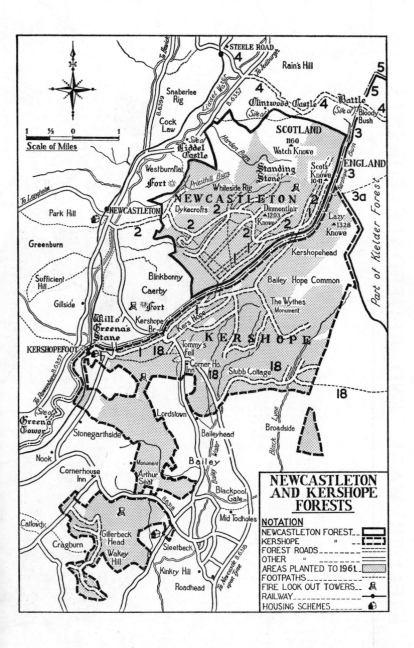

NEWCASTLETON
AND KERSHOPE
FORESTS

NOTATION
NEWCASTLETON FOREST
KERSHOPE   "
FOREST ROADS
OTHER   "
AREAS PLANTED TO 1961
FOOTPATHS
FIRE LOOK OUT TOWERS
RAILWAY
HOUSING SCHEMES

KIELDER, WARK AND REDESDALE FORESTS

OTTERBURN

Barrow Burn

ROMAN ROAD

A696

Dargues Burn

River Rede

Elishaw

Stewart Shiels

ROCHESTER
BREMENIUM

Roman Camp 1729

Sills

Sobbs

Woodlaw

Rooken

Ridlees Burn

Outer Golden Pot

Middle Golden Pot

Riddlesshope

Roman Camps

Pry Me

13

10

Featherwood

Coltonshopeburn

Coltonshope Foot

REDESDALE

Blackburnhead

ROMAN ROAD

The Pennine Way

Chew Green

Ravens Knowe

Ogre Hill

Spithope Head

Kielder Stone

BYRNESS

Blakehope Raw Hill

Blakehope

Blakehope Burnhaugh

Emblehope

9

ELLIS CRAG

Catcleugh Reservoir

Ramshope

8a 8a 8b 8b

8

Black

Woolmeath Edge

1723

Emblehope Moor

Carter Bar

Whitelee

A68

Ramshope Burn

Chattlehope Burn

7

Girdle Fell 1739

Oh Me Edge

Emblehope Moor

8

To Kelso

SCOTLAND 1898

ENGLAND

Carter Fell 1815

6e 6e 6e 6e

Knox Knowe 1636

6d Limestone Knowe 1601

Grey Mares Knowe 1691

6d

Kielder Head

7

Ridge End Burn

Three Pikes

To Hawick

6c 6c 6c

Part of Wauchope Forest

6b 6a

6a

Scaup Burn

Ridge End

Grey's Pike 1461

8

KIELDER

Peel Fell 1975

Mid Fell 1831

6a 6a 6a

6a 7 7

6a

Deadwater Fell 1867

Wheel Causey

Part of Wauchope Forest

Deadwater

Thorlieshope Pike 1160

Bells Linn

22 22

5

To Newcastleton
To Hawick

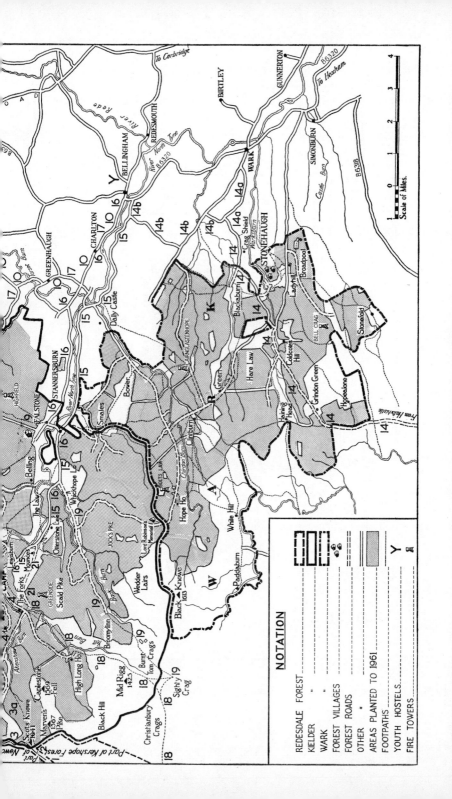

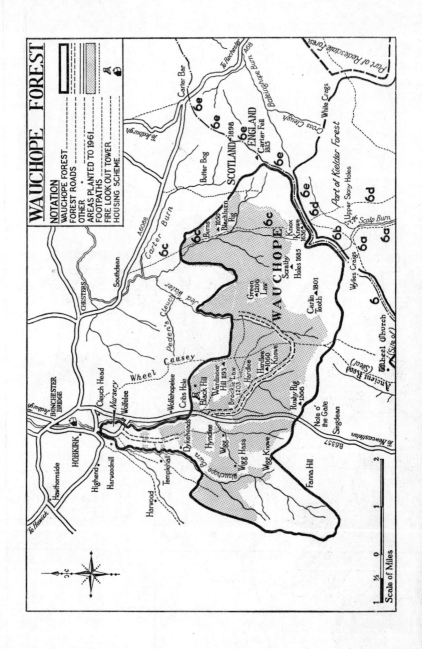

between the tributaries of the Jed Water in Scotland, and those of the Rede in England, climbs gradually to a height of 1,898 feet, and gives magnificent views over Redesdale, the green summits of the higher Cheviots to the north-east, and the broad valley of the Tweed. The only drawback is the character of the ground—a long succession of eroding peat-hags, passable but distinctly damp except in the finest of weather.

7. *Kielder to Catcleugh in Redesdale. Hill Walk, 14 miles.*
   (O.S. Sheet 70.)   Yellow signs.
   From the main entrance to Kielder Castle, take the tarred forest road indicated by the yellow signs, proceeding north-east up the Kielder Burn. Near Ridge End Farm, three miles up the dale, where the road forks, keep to the left, and follow the left-hand side of the stream to the isolated farmstead of Scalp, two miles further on. Proceed through the farmyard and cross a footbridge over the Scalp Burn. On the other side, bear right and follow the yellow signs through the farmstead of Kielder Head. The route now lies over open moorland on the western side of the White Kielder Burn. At the head of the dale it bears east (right-handed) and ascends steeply towards the summit of Girdle Fell, 1,739 feet, four miles from Scalp Farm. The recommended and marked route runs a little below the summit, to dodge boggy ground. Thence the path falls steeply down the valley of the Chattlehope Burn towards Catcleugh Reservoir, which may be seen plainly ahead, two miles beyond the summit of the pass. Turn right when the reservoir bank is reached, and follow it for a mile round to the dam, which is crossed to reach the main road (bus route) from Carter Bar to Otterburn. Turn right when this road is gained, to reach Byrness after two miles, or Rochester after a further five miles.

8. *Kielder or Lewisburn to Byrness. Hill Walk, 15 miles.*
   (O.S. Sheets 70 and 76.)   Red signs.
   At a point on the North Tyne road, two miles south of Kielder Castle and one mile north of the camp site, the old wooden Bakethin Bridge crosses the river. Take this and follow the forest road up the hill and under the railway bridge. Go on into the woods and follow the road round north-west to the edge of the older plantations, where it ends. There turn sharply north-east; follow first the edge of the older plantations and then a hill to the Mount Common fire tower. Continue north-east along the ride to Grey's Pike, following the edge of the young plantations. Half a mile beyond Grey's Pike descend north-west, following a ridge to the Kielder Burn. Cross this by the footbridge, and turn sharp right up the farm road to Ridge End Farm.

Alternatively, Ridge End Farm may be reached by the road up the Kielder Burn from Kielder Castle (yellow signs). This is the easier of the two routes, and the direct one from the Kielder Youth Hostel.

Go thence up the Ridge End Burn valley, ascending steadily for five miles to Blakehope Nick, nearly 1,500 feet above sea level. The route is marked by a ploughed furrow, drawn as a guide for tractors travelling on forestry work from one dale to the next. It descends from the Nick for four miles to the small-holding of Black Blakehope. Beyond this a forest road begins and immediately forks; take the left fork (**8a**) to strike the Otterburn-Carter Bar road at Byrness, three miles off. The right fork (**8b**, red signs) runs down the burn to Blakehopeburnhaugh. If one turns left there and crosses the bridge, it leads out on to the Carter Bar road at a point four miles north-west of Rochester.

9. *Falstone to Emblehope and Byrness. Hill Walk*, 12 *miles*.
(O.S. Sheets 70, 76 and 77.) Brown signs.

Leave the main road up the south bank of the River North Tyne, cross the river to Falstone Village, and go on to cross the railway. Just after crossing the railway, turn left and proceed uphill to the prominent whitewashed houses of Hawkhope Hill. Keeping to the right of these, take the track that bears right to run straight uphill to the fire lookout tower on Highfield Hill, three miles from the starting point; the telephone wires to this will serve as a guide.

Beyond the tower, which commands fine views over the forests, continue north along a ride for one mile to strike a gravelled forest road at the deserted homestead of Highfield Hope. Continue across this road, and drop slowly down along the ride to the deserted farm called The Dodd, in the valley of the Tarset Burn, which can be seen to the right. Thence the track continues north to cross the Smallhope Burn at a little school-house, long disused, which once served the children of farmers and shepherds on these scattered homesteads; it is said that the schoolmaster rode every day from Falstone by the track that we have followed.

Here the track leaves the woods and ahead, up the hill, can now clearly be seen the isolated farmstead of Emblehope, owned by the Duke of Northumberland, who breeds hardy black-faced sheep and hill cattle, and who has also planted about 600 acres of trees, partly for timber and partly as shelter for livestock. Proceeding beyond Emblehope, which is some six miles from Falstone, or two from Highfield Hope, the path bears to the right of a young spruce plantation, then heads into the valley of the Tarn Burn.

After crossing this, head due north towards the highest point on the skyline, Blackman's Law (1,501 feet). The path runs up a stream called the Long Sike, and then drops down Ralph's Clough to the farm of Black Blakehope in Redesdale Forest, and some four miles from Emblehope; there turn downstream, and on leaving the fields, either bear left for Byrness, two miles distant (**8a** on map) or continue downstream for Rochester, seven miles away (**8b** on map).

10. *Bellingham-Byrness, by Greenhaugh and Gib Shiel, public by-road, 19 miles.*

(O.S. Sheets 70 and 77.) Roads.

Although this route is open to cars and cycles, it is unfenced for much of the way, and untarred for a long stretch, while being little frequented it provides a pleasant route for walkers. Leave Bellingham by the Hexham road, but instead of turning left over the bridge, keep on the north side of the Tyne, following its course for four miles to Lanehead. There turn right for the pretty village of Greenhaugh, 1½ miles ahead. Half a mile beyond Greenhaugh, take a right fork, and about one mile further on, a right turn again. From this point there is a fine view north-west over the woods of Tarset Dale towards Emblehope Moor, while the road climbs for two miles past the plantations of High Green Moor.

Just beyond these, take a left turn to proceed north over Blackburn Common for two miles to the lonely shepherd's cottage at Gib Shiel.

A mile or so beyond this, the road crosses the slopes of Rooken Edge to enter the sprucewoods of Redesdale Forest, and a splendid panoramic view of Redesdale opens out, extending from Rochester over the outliers of the northern Cheviots towards Carter Bar. From a height of 1,140 feet the road drops steadily for four miles to Blakehopeburnhaugh. After crossing a Bailey bridge, bear right and cross a second bridge to emerge on the main road, one mile ahead; there a left turn leads to Byrness, two miles away, or a right turn to Rochester four miles distant.

WALKS WITHIN REDESDALE

11. *Low Byrness to Chew Green. Hill Walk, 7 miles.*

(O.S. Sheet: Scotland 86.) Brown signs.

Just opposite the forest offices beside the main road at Low Byrness, take the forest road up the Cottonshope Burn, and follow it until it emerges from the woods a mile ahead. Then go left-handed along the edge of the plantations, climbing a further mile to the fire look-out post on Byrness Hill, 1,338 feet. This gives a grand view over Redesdale and the Catcleugh Reservoir, with the new Byrness village looking like a set of doll's houses far away below.

Proceeding due north over the open fell, it is a simple matter to follow the watershed over Houx Hill and Raven Knowe (1,729 feet) to Ogre Hill, whence a track descends to the Border, only 3½ miles from Byrness hilltop.

You stand now at the headwaters of three rivers; southwards run tributaries of the Rede, towards the Tyne; to west and north a group of burns wind through the Leithope plantations, an outlying portion of Wauchope Forest, to form the Kale Water which feeds the Tweed; to the east the Coquet begins its meandering course through the Cheviots towards Rothbury and Amble. The Tweed basin stretches out to the north-west, while to the north-east the trackless green hills heave like waves of the sea towards the great square mass of The Cheviot, 2,676 feet high and twelve miles distant. Below, where the Border runs for a mile down the course of the Coquet, are laid out before you the bold rectangular outlines of the great Roman camp of Chew Green, at a key point where the Roman road from Rochester to Newsteads follows its high-level route over the Cheviots. An easy drop of 1½ miles leads you into the actual camp.

This route runs just in the safety zone to the west of a firing range, and during the summer months it is unsafe to attempt any return that leads farther *east*. The best return route from the camp is that south-west along the Border watershed for three miles over the hill called the Heart's Toe (Norse, *hjort's tue*, hart's knoll), to Greyhound Law, to meet Path **12** described below.

12. *Byrness to the Border Line. Hill Walk, 3 miles.*
(O.S. Sheet 70.)   Yellow signs.
From the new Byrness village, walk along the main road for ¼ mile towards Carter Bar. Then take the forest road on the right, keeping to the right of Hawkhope Nick, and head for a cairn on the ridge. Follow this ridge till the Border is reached at the top of Greyhound Law, 1,587 feet.

13. *Bremenium, ¾ mile from main road.*
(O.S. Sheet 70.)   Road.
The Roman station of Bremenium or High Rochester is best reached by taking the by-road which diverges from the main road a quarter of a mile south-east of Rochester, close to a war memorial. Besides the Roman walls and gateways, the visitor should note an old peel tower, still occupied, standing within the encampment.

Blackhope, Forest Road and Track, 6 miles.
(O.S. Sheet 70.)   Tracks.
From the forest office at Low Byrness, walk half a mile east towards Rochester, then take a forest road on the right and cross the first of two Bailey bridges. Turn right (following red signs along

part of route **8b**) and go on through spruce plantations to the holding of Black Blakehope, deep amid the woods. Just before the steading is reached, a minor forest track (**8a**), with blue signs, springs off to the right. This leads over Tod Law, gives a good view of Upper Redesdale and Byrness village, and emerges on the main road by the old Byrness Church, one mile from the starting point.

A TRAMP THROUGH WARK FOREST

14. *Haltwhistle to Wark* (16 *miles*) *or Bellingham* (19½ *miles*).
(O.S. Sheets 76 and 77.) Yellow signs on forest lands.

The best line of access from the south is that via Grindon Green. From Town Foot, at the east end of Haltwhistle, go north for 1¼ miles to the direct Newcastle-Greenhead main road. Turn right and follow this for one mile; then turn left along a road signposted "Cowburn", crossing the Roman Wall half a mile on, and reaching a road junction half a mile still further on. At this point a by-road from the Once Brewed Youth Hostel, which avoids main road work, comes in from the east. We keep left and go north for three miles to Robin Rock Drift farm. Thence a track goes 1½ miles north, swings north-east, reaches Grindon Green cottage another mile on, and shortly enters Wark Forest. Three miles of forest road leads eastward downhill to Whygate, where country roads are rejoined, close to a ford and footbridge over the Warks Burn. Bearing left, take the one that follows the north side of the Warks Burn (the other leads to Simonburn).

About 1½ miles further on, where the road leaves the woods, the new village of Stonehaugh may be seen half a mile to the right. During the next 2½ miles of pleasant downhill walking, note the strategic siting of three or four isolated farmsteads, standing no doubt where old peel towers once dominated the land. At the next fork, turn right for Wark village, 2½ miles (**14a**). For Bellingham, (**14b**) 6 miles, turn left, left again after one mile, and follow the road where it swings right 1½ miles farther on, to cross Ealingham Rigg, with its fine view of Tyne and Rede valleys, and then to descend into North Tynedale, where Bellingham nestles amid the sycamores.

ROUTES FROM BELLINGHAM TO THE
KIELDER CAMP SITE AND YOUTH HOSTEL
(O.S. Sheets 70, 76 and 77.)

15. *Main Road* (15 *miles to Camp Site*).

The main road up the North Tyne valley follows the *south* bank. It is reached from Bellingham by crossing the river at the main bridge, and turning right. It is the best route for cars, being ungated.

16. *Secondary Road* (15 *miles*).

The secondary road keeps to the *north* bank of the Tyne. Do not cross the river on leaving Bellingham, but go straight on to Lanehead and continue by the gated road to Falstone. Here cross the river and turn right on to the south bank road. Open to cars.

The Youth Hostel is two miles beyond the Camp Site in each case, and is reached by following the main road north-west to the old railway viaduct, then diverging right.

17. *Bellingham to the Lewisburn Camp Site via the Forest Road through Waterhead and Plashetts. Hill Road,* 16 *miles.*

(O.S. Sheets 70, 76 and 77.)   Pink signs on forest lands.

This makes a grand hill walk, but is rather too steep for cyclists; after the first few miles the tarmac is left, and gravel roads continue. Follow Route **10** through Lanehead (4 miles) and Greenhaugh; bear right (signposted High Green) after leaving Greenhaugh. Then at the next road junction, beside Diamond Cottage, turn left (signposted The Comb). Thorneyburn Church may be seen beside the woods to the left, and the road soon passes through the hamlet of Greenhaugh, six miles from Bellingham. Here there are two (yes, two!) fine old peels or fortified farmhouses, one in ruins, the other well preserved and showing a well-defended raised entrance to its upper living quarters; the ground floor, which was used as a byre for the cattle, has a narrow entrance and was also defensible.

Follow the road on, and over a ford, until sign posts saying "Border Forest Park" are reached at Waterhead, eight miles from Bellingham. Here turn left and cross a Bailey bridge. (The other road leads to Emblehope). Once over this bridge, it is a simple matter to follow the gravel road right through the woods to Plashetts, seven miles away. Just beyond the bridge, note on the right the ruins of an old peel called Barty's Castle; another ruined peel called Corbie Castle lies about a mile beyond this, down by the burn side. Beyond the farmsteads of Highfield and Highfield Hope the road crosses a minor ridge called The Cross, and an amazing panorama of the North Tyne valley suddenly opens out. Deadwater Fell is prominent to the north-west, and just to the left of it some of the Scottish hills are visible, including Cauldcleuch Head, 1,996 feet, beyond Wauchope Forest.

The road now drops down past a shepherd's steading called Belling Burn Head, to the sad, uninhabited, deserted colliery village of Plashetts. Here, beside the ruins of a church and a chapel, may be seen the dwellings of the miners who once worked a flourishing colliery. A little coal is still mined from a drift which opens just below the road. Beyond this point the road drops steeply to the modern hamlet of Plashetts, crosses below the railway by a low bridge, and proceeds over two Bailey bridges, the second being over the North Tyne. It then emerges on the main road up the North Tyne valley. Turn right to reach the main entrance to the Lewisburn camp site, half a mile further on.

(When taking this route in the reverse direction, remember to turn sharp right just after crossing *under* the low bridge at Plashetts; thereafter the road is easily followed.)

18. *Lewisburn to Christianbury Crags and Kershopefoot. Hill Walk, 21 miles.*

(O.S. Sheet 76.)   Red signs.

This provides a strenuous but attractive hike for the serious walker who is expert at way-finding. From the camp site, cross the main road and follow the Bloody Bush route (No. **4** on map) for two miles as far as the first farm, called The Forks. There cross the bridge, then turn left up the hill; follow the forest road for three miles until it ends just beyond the farm of High Long House. Follow the stream uphill for half a mile; then, where it forks, ford the Lishaw Burn, and follow the other branch, called the Yett Burn, almost due south into the hills.

Head for the skyline, four miles away, aiming to reach it at Burnt Tom Crags (1,621 feet) on the Forest Park Boundary, and also on the border of Northumberland and Cumberland. Here you should see a path, marked with brown signs, running to Sighty Crag (1,702 feet) which lies ¾ mile south, and so round to Route **19**, described below.

But for Kershopefoot, proceed due west, following the *red* signs to Christianbury Crags, 1½ miles on. These crags give a wonderful view towards the Solway, with Kershope Forest in the middle distance. They are famous as the home of a herd of wild goats.

The route from Christianbury Crags lies almost due west and steadily downhill for three miles towards the southern corner of the Kershope sprucewoods. Only a path runs through the heather, but the woods are visible for most of the way. Be careful to avoid wandering *southwards*, as that leads only into a trackless waste used as a firing zone. Enter the woods by a ride, which shortly becomes a gravelled road and crosses the Black Lyne river by a modern bridge. Then follow this road through the forest for two miles, bearing left at each road junction, to emerge on the tarred *public* road near Baileyhead.

Turn right, and proceed for two miles to the Dog and Gun Inn. There turn right again, and follow the tarred country road downhill for one mile to Kershope Bridge. Do not cross this, but instead turn left and follow the gravel *forest* road downstream for 1½ miles to a second bridge over the Kershope Burn. Again do not cross the stream, but turn left on to the county road and ascend a slope; after a few hundred yards turn right to proceed downhill for one mile to Kershope Station. The Newcastleton-Canonbie road lies just beyond.

Since there are no artificial landmarks, and no shelter, between High Long House and the Black Lyne Woods, this walk should be undertaken only in clear, fair weather.

19. *From Emmethaugh up the Whickhope Burn to Sighty Crags and Christianbury Crags. Hill Walk, 8 miles out. (25 miles round from camp site.)*

(O.S. Sheet 76.)   Brown signs.

Emmethaugh lies on the main road up the North Tyne, some two miles west of Falstone and 4½ miles east of the Lewisburn camp site. Here a modern bridge spans the Whickhope Burn, and close by a signpost saying 'Whickhope' points the way up this outstandingly beautiful though remote valley. After passing two or three farmsteads and a group of Forest Workers Holdings, the road enters the spruce woods after 2¼ miles, near the farmstead called Cranecleugh. Follow the signposts saying 'Broomy Linn' to the deserted farm of that name—the last one up the dale, 2½ miles farther on. Then go ahead over the moors, following first the main burn and then, where that swings away to the left, a tributary stream. Head for the Grey Mare's Crags, 1,498 feet, which may be seen on the skyline, two miles from Broomy Linn farm. Keep to the high ridge and proceed in the same direction for a further mile to Sighty Crag. This lies half a mile beyond the Park's boundary, and with its 1,702 feet elevation is the highest point in the long range of hills (sometimes called the Bewcastle Fells) that parts the North Tyne valley from the low ground of Cumberland.

For an alternative return route, strike north west along the ridge to Burnt Tom Crags, 1,629 feet, just over a mile away. Then, again following the ridge, bear west for Christianbury Crags, 1½ miles farther on. From this landmark one may return by route **18** above (taken in reverse) down the Lishaw Burn to High Long House and the forest road to Lewisburn.

Since there are only indefinite shepherds' tracks after leaving the forest roads, this walk should be attempted only in good weather, and a one-inch map and compass should be regarded as essential items of equipment.

20. *Fernyknowe, 6 miles.*

Leave the camp site by the Kielder road. Just after crossing the Lewis Burn, turn off left up a forest road marked with a brown signs and follow this round Ferny Knowe Hill until you meet another forest road, three miles on. Here turn right, and follow yellow signs downhill to the main road at Bewshaugh. Here another right turn leads back to the camp site.

21. *Mounces, 6 miles.*

Follow route **18** as far as The Forks farm, but do not cross the river there. Instead, turn left and follow the forest road (blue signs) over to Mounces, where the county road is met. A left turn leads back to the camp. (6 miles).

22. *Crag Head, 7 miles.*

Go north along the county road to the forest workshop at Lewie. There strike off left, and follow a forest road with white signs through the woods for three miles. Near Crag Head there are fine views of Deadwater Moor and the Scottish hills. The route drops down east to strike the county road at the Old Manse, where a right turn leads back to the camp. (7 miles).

THE ROAD ROUTE FROM THE CAMP SITE TO WAUCHOPE, CARTER BAR, AND REDESDALE

Take the road north-west past Kielder to reach the Border at Deadwater. The road then continues down the River Liddel to the hamlet of Saughtree. Here turn *sharp* right and climb the steep Note o' the Gate Pass. At one point a grand view opens out to the left; Peel Fell and Deadwater Fell dominate the landscape, with the broad expanse of sprucewoods in the North Tyne Valley visible beyond.

Over the pass, the broad vistas of the Scottish Borders open out, as the road (B6357) falls through Wauchope Forest. On reaching the main road (A6038) turn right for Carter Bar, and follow A68 to Redesdale Forest.

BOOKS OF
THE BORDER COUNTRY

The following lists have been compiled with the kind assistance of the Librarians in the district.

BOOKS ON NORTHUMBERLAND

SELECTED BY MISS R. E. BAKER
County Librarian, Morpeth

ARMSTRONG, JAMES. *Wanny Blossoms; A Book of Song.* Poems of Tynedale and Redesdale. 1879.

BAKER, J. G. and G. R. TATE. A new flora of Northumberland and Durham. (*Trans. Nat. Hist. Soc. Northumb.* 1867. Vol. 2, pp. 1-316).

BATES, CADWALLADER, J. *The History of Northumberland.* 1895.

BOLAM, GEORGE. *Birds of Northumberland.* 1912.

BRADLEY, A. G. *The Romance of Northumberland.* 1933.

BRADLEY, A. G. *The Gateway of Scotland.* 1912.

BRITISH ASSOCIATION. *Scientific survey of north-eastern England.* 1949.

CHAPMAN, ABEL. *Bird-Life of the Borders.* 1889.

CHAPMAN, ABEL. *The Borders and Beyond.* 1924.

DIXON, DAVID DIPPIE. *Upper Coquetdale, Northumberland.* 1903.

DIXON, DAVID DIPPIE. *Whittingham Vale, Northumberland.* 1895.

FOLK-LORE SOCIETY. *County folk-lore.* Vol. IV. Collected by M. C. Balfour, edited by Northcote W. Thomas. 1904.

GRAHAM, P. ANDERSON. *Highways and byways in Northumbria.* 1921.

HESLOP, RICHARD OLIVER. *Northumberland words: a glossary.* 2 Vols. 1892-1894.

HODGSON, JOHN. *A history of Northumberland.* 7 Vols. 1820-58.

HONEYMAN, HERBERT L. *Northumberland* (County Books Series). 1949.

HOUSE, JOHN WILLIAM. *Bellingham and Wark, a comparative study.* 1953.

HOUSE, JOHN WILLIAM. *Population structure and employment conditions.* 1952.

HOUSE, JOHN WILLIAM. *Migration and employment among school leavers and young adults.* 1931-50.

HUGILL, ROBERT. *Borderland castles and peles.* 1939.

JERNINGHAM, HUBERT E. H. *Norham Castle.* 1883.

MACK, JAMES LOGAN. *The Border line.* 1924.

MAWER, ALAN. *The place-names of Northumberland and Durham.* 1920.

MEE, ARTHUR. *Northumberland.* (King's England). 1952.

MORRIS, J. E. *Northumberland.* (Little Guides). 1933.

NORTHUMBERLAND COUNTY HISTORY COMMITTEE. *A history of Northumberland.* 15 Vols. 1893-1940.

RAINE, JAMES. *The history and antiquities of North Durham.* 1852.

RICHARDON, M. A. *Local Historian's Table Book.* Circa. 1844.

SHARP, THOMAS. *Northumberland:* a Shell guide. New edition. 1954.

SYKES. *Local Records.*

TEGNER, HENRY. *A Border county;* an account of its wild life. 1955.

TOMLINSON, WILLIAM WEAVER. *Comprehensive guide to the County of Northumberland.* 10th edition. 1923.

TREVELYAN, GEORGE MACAULAY. "The Middle Marches". (In *Clio, a muse, and other essays*).

WHITTAKER, W. G. ed. *North countrie ballads, songs and pipe-tunes.* 2 parts. 1921.

WILSON, J. M. *Tales of the Borders, and of Scotland.* 3 Vols. 1880.

BOOKS ON THE
KERSHOPE FOREST REGION OF CUMBERLAND

SELECTED BY KENNETH SMITH
City Librarian, Carlisle

Topography, History

BAIN, JOSEPH ed. *The Border Papers.* 1560-1603. 2 vols. 1894-6.

BOGG, EDMUND. *A Thousand miles of wandering in the Border Country.* 1898 (pp. 288 ff.).

FERGUSON, R. S. *A History of Cumberland.* 1890.

FERGUSON, R. S. "Liddel Moat". (*in Transactions Cumberland & Westmorland Antiquarian Society,* Old Series, Vol. 9. 1888, pp. 404-408.

HODGKIN, DR. THOMAS. *The Wardens of the Northern Marches.* (J. Murray 1908).

HUTCHINSON WILLIAM. *The History of the County of Cumberland.* 2 vols. 1794.

JEFFERSON SAMUEL. *The History and Antiquities of Cumberland.* Vol. 1 Leath Ward. 1840.

NANSON, WILLIAM. Bewcastle. (*in Trans. Cumb. & West. Ant. and Arch. Soc.,* Old Series, 1878. Vol. 3, pp. 215 ff.).

NICHOLSON, JOSEPH AND RICHARD BURN. *The History and Antiquities of the counties of Westmorland and Cumberland.* 2 vols. 1777.

PEASE, HOWARD. *The Lord Wardens of the Marches of England and Scotland.*

TOPPING, GEORGE. *Rambles in Borderland with 'the Clan'.* 1921.

WILSON, JAMES (ed.). *Victoria History of Cumberland.* 1905. 2 vols.

Natural History

HODGSON, WILLIAM. "The Hill Naturalist". (*in Transactions of the Cumberland and Westmorland Association for the Advancement of Literature and Science,* Vol. XI, 1885-86, pp. 13-39).

HODGSON, WILLIAM. *Flora of Cumberland.* 1898. Map.

MACPHERSON, H. A. and WILLIAM DUCKWORTH. *The Birds of Cumberland.* 1886.

Literature

ELLWOOD, REV. T. "The Poets and Poetry of Cumberland", (*in Trans. of the Cum. & West. Assn. for Advancement of Lit. and Sci.,* Vol. IX, 1883-84, pp. 137-167.)

HAMILTON, LORD ERNEST WILLIAM. *The Outlaws of the Marches.* 1897.

PEASE, HOWARD. *With the Warden of the Marches; or, The Vow by the 'Nine Stane Rig'.* 1909.

SCOTT, SIR WALTER. *The Black Dwarf,* 1816 (Scene—the Lowlands and the Border, *circa* 1706).

SCOTT, SIR WALTER. *Guy Mannering,* 1815 (Contains description of wild country between the Lyne and Irthing).

BOOKS ON BORDER HISTORY AND ROXBURGHSHIRE

SELECTED BY MISS R. M. McIVOR
Hawick Public Library

AINSWORTH, BERNARD. *Teviotside legends and stories.* 1895.

ALISON, JAMES P. *The Hermitage Chapel.* 1901.

ANDERSON, DAVID. *Musings by the burns and braes of Liddesdale.* 1868.

ARMSTRONG, ROBERT BRUCE. *The History of Liddesdale, Eskdale, Ewesdale, Wauchopedale and the Debateable Land.* 1883.

BANKS, F. R. *Scottish Border Country.* 1951.

BEATTIE, DAVID J. *Lang syne in Eskdale.* 1950.

Border Pamphlets: *Liddesdale. Hermitage Castle; A national forest in Liddesdale; Liddesdale; Newcastleton; A Border village; and Hermitage Castle* (2).

BORLAND, R. *Border raids and reivers.* III. Tom Scott. 1910.

BOYD, HALBERT J. *Kinmont Willie.* 1934. (Fiction).

Calendar of Border papers. 2 vols. 1560-1603. Edited J. BAIN. 1894-96.

CARRE, WALTER RIDDELL. *Border Memories.* 1876.

DOUGLAS, SIR GEORGE. *A history of the Border counties* (Roxburgh, Selkirk, Peebles). 1899.

EDDINGTON, ALEXANDER. *Castles and historic homes of the Border.* 1926.

GRAHAM, JOHN. *Conditions of the Border at the Union.* 1905.

HALL, WILLIAM. *Liddesdale.* 1903.

JEFFREY, ALEXANDER. *An historical and descriptive account of Roxburghshire.* 1918.

LAWRIE, WILLIAM H. *Border river angling.* 1946.

MALONEY, WILLIAM J. *George and John Armstrong of Castleton.* 1954.

NEW STATISTICAL ACCOUNT OF SCOTLAND. Vol. 3—Roxburgh—Peebles—Selkirk. 1845.

OGILVIE, WILL H. *Poems.* 1923-30.

OLIVER, J. R. *Upper Teviotdale and the Scotts of Buccleuch.* 1887.

OLIVER, J. R. *Border sketches.* 1904.

PLATT, WILLIAM and MRS. *Stories of the Scottish Border.* 1917.

ROBSON, JAMES. *Churches and churchyards of Teviotdale.* 1893.

SPARROW, W. SHAW, ed. *In the Border country.* III. by James Orrock with historical notes by W. S. Crockett. 1906.

STEWART, DUNCAN. *The Covenanters of Teviotdale and neighbouring districts.* 1908.

TANCRED, GEORGE. *Annals of a Border Club.* 1899.

TAYLOR, R. M. *Teviot reaches.* (Sketches and etchings) 1951.

VEITCH, JOHN. *The history and poetry of the Scottish Border.* 2 vols. 1893.

WATSON, GEORGE. *The Roxburghshire word-book.* 1923.

Among recent works we would mention *Liddesdale, Historical and Descriptive*, written by JOHN BYERS, a native of Newcastleton, and published in 1952, price 15/- by John MacQueen, 27 Channel St., Galashiels.

GENERAL INFORMATION

The visitor to the Border Forest Park must bear in mind that it occupies one of the least accessible regions of Britain. Roads are few and far between, public transport services are limited, and there are no large tourist centres with ample hotel accommodation. The remoteness of the district, with its wide expanses of windswept fells rising high above the spreading spruce woods and the fringe of farmlands along the dales, is however one of the leading attractions to those who come from populous cities. Provided they remember the big distances that lie between one road, or village with lodging accommodation, and the next, they will find their travels both enjoyable and rewarding. But the Border Forest Park is definitely *not* a place where there is a tea room round every corner; even shops are few and far between and the visitor is well advised to carry a packed snack or sandwiches on a trip of any duration.

All visitors to the Park are expected to observe the well-known Country Code, to leave no litter, close all gates, and above all to exercise especial care with matches, tobacco, and fire in any form. The Border Forests are a priceless reserve of growing timber but are particularly vulnerable, during dry weather, to fire risk.

ACCESS BY RAIL

Two railway routes run close to the Park, although only one actually touches on it. This is the well-known Waverley Route from London to Edinburgh, which runs via Carlisle and Hawick. All expresses stop at both those stations, and the run up Liddesdale affords fine views of the plantations in both Kershope and Newcastleton Forests.

Local trains stop at the following stations: Penton and Kershopefoot, near Kershope Forest; Newcastleton and Steele Road, giving access to Newcastleton Forest: and at Riccarton Junction, from which the western end of Kielder Forest may be reached by a hill track. Only Kershopefoot and Newcastleton Stations, however, lie really close to the woods.

The second railway route is that which crosses England from Newcastle to Carlisle. Hexham, where expresses stop, and from which there are through connections to London via Newcastle, is the most convenient centre, from which buses may be taken to Wark and to Bellingham for Kielder Forest. Other stations at

Haydon Bridge, Bardon Mill, Haltwhistle, Greenhead, and Gilsland may serve as jumping-off points for Wark Forest or the Roman Wall.

The various branch lines shown on old maps as serving Bellingham, Kielder Forest, and the Rothbury and Kirkwhelpington districts, are no longer in use.

These are limited, and are best considered under the component forests of the Park.

Kielder and Wark

(1) Daily service (about 12 buses each day) from Hexham to Wark and Bellingham. Operated by Messrs. Mid-Tyne Transport Ltd., (M. Charlton & Sons.), The Garage, Acomb, near Hexham. (Phone: Hexham 217); timetables available free of charge (3d. post free).

(2) Daily service (about 4 buses each day) from Newcastle to Wark and Bellingham, operated by Messrs. Mid-Tyne Transport Ltd., (M. Charlton & Sons), as above.

(3) Hexham itself may be reached from Newcastle and most other towns in Northumberland and Durham by the various routes of United Automobile Services, Ltd., of United House, Grange Road, Darlington. Timetables 1s. (1s. 6d. post free). This company also operates a service to Haltwhistle, Gilsland, and Carlisle, which may be of assistance when visiting Wark Forest or the Roman Wall.

(4) An infrequent bus service operates between Bellingham and Kielder on weekdays only, and on Mondays and Saturdays it is extended to Saughtree and Steele Road Station (connections by rail from Hawick and Carlisle). From Kielder to Bellingham the first morning bus leaves at 8 a.m. (6.30 a.m. and 11 a.m. on Mondays and Saturdays only) arriving Bellingham one hour later. On Mondays and Saturdays there are buses from Bellingham to Kielder at 7.45 a.m., 2.30 p.m., and 6.30 p.m. (These are the current times as we go to press) All the Bellingham buses connect with those of M. Charlton & Sons, running into Hexham. There is no Sunday service to Kielder. Details of the service are obtainable from the operator, Mr. Norman Fox, Falstone, Hexham.

Redesdale

A long-distance bus service runs on A.68 from Newcastle to Otterburn, Rochester, and Byrness, and then on to Jedburgh and

Edinburgh; there are two buses each day in summer, one in winter. At Jedburgh, a connection may be made for Glasgow; one bus daily. Details from United Automobile Services, Darlington. Or from Scottish Omnibuses (S.M.T. Ltd., of New Street, Edinburgh), time tables 3d. (6d. post free); this Company also serves Jedburgh.

Wauchope Forest

The nearest bus route to the eastern portion of this forest, and its camp site at Burns Cottage, is the Redesdale one shown above; this passes Carter Bar, 3 miles from the entrance road to the camp site. The nearest regular bus service to the western portion of the forest—Bonchester Bridge, is that run by Andersons (see foot of p. 97).

Kershope and Newcastleton Forests

Daily bus services operated by Western S.M.T. run from Carlisle, Annan, or Dumfries, via Canonbie, to Langholm. From Canonbie there are connections on Saturdays and Sundays to Kershopefoot and Newcastleton town. Timetables 3d. (6d. post free) from Western S.M.T. Co., Carlisle.

HOTEL ACCOMMODATION

The nearest centres with several large hotels are Hexham, Carlisle and Hawick. At places nearer to the Forest Park, hotels are smaller and fewer in number, and at holiday times it is advisable to book accommodation well in advance. The names of some of the main licensed hotels with lodging accommodation within reach of the Park are set out below. The figure in brackets is the distance, in miles, from each hotel to the nearest portion of the Park.

Hexham (12). Royal, County, Beaumont.
Wall (8). Hadrian.
Wark (4). Battlesteads, Black Bull.
Chollerton, George, Barrasford Arms.
Bellingham (3). Railway.
Falstone (0). Blackcock.
Otterburn (6). Percy Arms, Otterburn Tower, Otterburn Hall.
Woodburn (7). Fox and Hounds, Bay Horse.
Bonchester Bridge (1). Wolfelee, Horse and Hound.
Byrness (0). Byrness Hotel.
Rochester (1). Redesdale Arms.
Greenhead (6). Greenhead Hotel.
Gilsland (8). Station.
Brampton (10). White Lion, Sands House.

Carlisle (20). County and Station, Crown and Mitre, Red Lion, Central, Viaduct.

Langholm (10). Ashley Bank, Buck, Crown, Eskdale.

Longtown (8). Graham Arms.

Canonbie (6). Cross Keys.

Newcastleton (1). Grapes, Liddesdale.

Hawick (7). Buccleuch, Crown, Tower, Teviotdale Lodge, Victoria.

Jedburgh (20). Royal, Spread Eagle.

YOUTH HOSTELS

On the English side of the Border the nearest Youth Hostels, with distances in miles from the Forest Park, are the following:

(1) Kielder (0) (close to railway viaduct near Kielder Castle).

(2) Bellingham (3).

(3) Wholehope, near Alwinton (6).

(4) Acomb, near Hexham (10).

(5) Once Brewed, near Bardon Mill, Haltwhistle (7).

(6) Carlisle, (20).

Further details will be found in the Handbook of the Youth Hostels Association (England and Wales) obtainable from the Secretary, Welwyn Garden City, Herts. price 9d. (1s. post free).

In Scotland the only Youth Hostels within walking distance of the Park are:

(1) Snoot, near Hawick (12).

(2) Ferniehirst, near Jedburgh (18).

Full information will be found in the Scottish Youth Hostels Association Handbook, obtainable from the Secretary, 7, Bruntsfield Crescent, Edinburgh 10, price 1s. (1s. 5d. post free).

CAMP SITES

A. LEWISBURN CAMPING GROUND, KIELDER FOREST

The camp adjoins the Bellingham-Saughtree road and is approached by the North Tyne road. A hard road leads off the county road about two miles south of Kielder, turning north into the camp site. The Lewis Burn and the River North Tyne flow alongside the site. O.S. one-inch map. Sheet 76. Nat. Grid Ref. NY. 650904.

No advance booking of sites is required. Enquiries to: The Warden, Lewisburn Camp Site, Kielder, near Hexham, Northumberland. Phone: Kielder 229.

The Warden runs a small shop for the sale of tobacco, confectionery, postcards and some packed and tinned food, etc. Travelling shops pass close to the site several times a week but visitors are strongly advised to take some provisions with them, as the nearest shops are at Falstone—7 miles—and Bellingham—fifteen miles away. Supplies of milk can be arranged with the Warden. Motorists should note that the nearest petrol pump is seven miles away at Stannersburn near Falstone. Milk can be obtained locally.

Charges at Site A. are:

Car and tent or caravan: 4s. per day (or part of a day); or 24s. per week.

Motor cycle and tent: 2s. 6d. per day; 15s. per week.

Tent alone: 1s. per day; 6s. per week.

Day parking: 1s. per vehicle per day; coaches only by arrangement.

These charges include hot and cold water, and toilet facilities, and the use of a recreation pavilion with common room, verandah and drying room. Electricity is available for cooking and washing up, but not for caravan connections.

B. BURNTSHIELDS CAMPING SITE. KERSHOPE FOREST

A small camping ground with space for 20 tents, a water supply, but no other facilities, is situated half a mile south of Kershope. Best reached by taking the Canonbie—Newcastleton road (B6357) to Under Burnmouth, 3 miles south of Newcastleton; there turn east, pass the Kershopefoot Station, turn left at first fork, sharp right at next fork: road winds sharply and steeply uphill to site on left of road. Trains at Kershopefoot Station, 2 miles by forest track. Nat. Grid Ref. NY. 506831; O.S. Sheet 76.

This site is ¼ mile north of the Dog and Gun public house, marked "Corner House" on the one-inch map. Plans are in hand for the possible development of a larger site, closer to Kershopefoot Station.

C. BURNS COTTAGE CAMPING SITE. WAUCHOPE FOREST

Another small site, holding up to 10 tents but no caravans, lies off the Hawick—Carter Bar—Newcastle road (A6088) at Southdean. Turn south down a forest road, 3½ miles west-north-west of Carter Bar. Nat. Grid Ref. NT. 650060; O.S. Sheet 70. The Edinburgh—Jedburgh—Newcastle bus service passes Carter Bar, 3½ miles distant. Trains at Hawick. 11 miles. Local bus from Hawick to Bonchester Bridge (4 miles), and on Saturdays to Chesters Crossroads (2 miles), operated by Thomas Anderson, Bonchester Bridge. (Phone: Bonchester Bridge 203). This site lies 1½ miles down a forest road, close to an old cottage by a stream.

Charges at Sites B and C are:
    Car and tent, 3s. per day, 18s. per week; motor cycle and tent,
    2s. per day, 12s. per week; tent alone, 9d. per day, 4s. 6d.
    per week.

D. CAMPING SITE FOR YOUTH ORGANISATIONS

A site with a water supply, but no other facilities, has been
reserved beside the Lewis Burn, near Site A above. It is available
without charge provided prior booking has been made with the
Conservator of Forests for North-East England, Briar House,
Fulford Road, York.

All the sites are open from April 1st (or Easter if earlier) to 30th
September each year.

ROADS

Visitors usually approach the Park by one of four routes that give
wonderful views of its forest and moorland scenery. These are:

(1) The North Tyne Road from Chollerford and Bellingham, north-
west through Wark Forest and Kielder Forest, past the Lewisburn
camp site and Kielder Village, and on across the Border into
Liddesdale. To reach Chollerford, a well-known road junction near
Chollerton, take A69 and B6318 *west* from Newcastle; or else take
A69 and B6318 *east* from Carlisle; or else take A6079 *north* from
Hexham. From Chollerton, follow B6320 north towards Bellingham;
just before Bellingham, diverge west for Kielder.

(2) The main Redesdale road (A696 and A68) from Newcastle
and Otterburn, which goes north-west through Redesdale Forest,
passes Byrness Village, and crosses over into Scotland at Carter
Bar, to descend past Wauchope Forest at Bonchester Bridge, on
its way to Hawick (A6088).

(3) The main road A7 from Carlisle to Canonbie; thence by
B6357 north up Liddesdale, this road touches on Kershope Forest
near Kershopefoot Station, and Newcastleton Forest at the town
of Newcastleton, and goes on to cross the high and wild Note o' the
Gate Pass, to Bonchester Bridge and Hawick or Jedburgh.

(4) From the north, Jedburgh is the most convenient starting
point. Follow the A68 south-east for Carter Bar and Redesdale.
Near Otterburn take B6320 south for Bellingham and the North
Tyne. Alternatively, 2 miles south of Jedburgh, take B6357 south-
west for Bonchester Bridge. Then A6088 and B6357 again for
Wauchope Forest and Liddesdale. At Saughtree, a by-road runs
east for Kielder, Lewisburn Camp, and the North Tyne.

Wark Forest can only be approached by car along by-roads from Simonburn, Wark, or Bellingham.

A glance at the maps will show that big distances lie between the few roads that give access to the various portions of the Forest Park. Connecting links for motors are few and far between, and a round tour to take in two or three forests involves a long mileage. One useful cross-route is that from Bellingham to Otterburn, which links Kielder Forest with Redesdale.

The minor public roads vary considerably in character and surface, and one or two shown on the quarter-inch Ordnance Survey map are barely passable to motor cars. In particular the route from Newcastleton to Kielder via Bloody Bush, and that from Haltwhistle via Grindon Green, are quite unsuitable for ordinary cars. But in general the motorist will find most of the side roads satisfactory, though some are gated and few are free from stray sheep.

The network of new *forest* roads is not open to private cars, as the needs of protection from forest fires, and of timber haulage, must come first. Walkers, however, are welcome to use them; though during periods of exceptional fire hazard it may become necessary to close those routes that are not public rights of way.

SHOPS

In the main Kielder Valley, along the North Tyne, there are shops at Wark, Bellingham, Falstone and the Lewisburn camp site. One close to the old Kielder Forest Station is open for part of the day only. Also near the valley, there are shops at Greenhaugh, and at Lanehead, close to Tarset. The nearest petrol station to the camp site is at Stannersburn.

In Redesdale, there are shops at Otterburn, Rochester, Byrness and West Woodburn, and a petrol station at Byrness. The nearest shop to Wauchope Forest is at Bonchester Bridge.

In Liddesdale, there are shops at Newcastleton, at Kershopefoot, and just south of Liddel Park.

INNS

In addition to the hotels with lodging accommodation listed earlier, there is an inn (Dog and Gun) close to Kershope Forest at the point marked on the one-inch Ordnance Map as Corner House, three miles east of Kershopefoot; and also at another point marked Corner House four miles south of Kershopefoot.

Beside Kielder Forest, there are inns at Greenhaugh, north of Tarset; at Greystone, and at Stannersburn.

The local forest offices, where visitors may obtain information regarding work in progress and the best means of seeing the woods and the countryside, are situated as follows:

There are forest offices for *Kielder* at Kielder Castle, Kielder Camp, Plashetts, Whickhope, Stannersburn and Greenhaugh, for *Wark* at Stonehaugh village and The Bower, Tarset, and for *Redesdale* at Low Byrness, one mile east of Byrness village.

The office for *Wauchope* Forest is close to the new houses at Bonchester Bridge; that for *Newcastleton* Forest is at Dykecrofts, 1½ miles east of Newcastleton Town; and that for *Kershope* Forest is beside Kershopefoot Station.

GOLF

There is a golf club at Bellingham, open to visitors.

TENNIS

There is a club at Kielder; enquiries regarding visitors' tickets should be made at the Castle.

HORSE RIDING

The forest roads and some of the tracks over the open fells form excellent trails for riders and pony trekkers.

FISHING

On the River Rede, a stretch is held by the Byrness Angling Club, and enquiries may be made of the Head Forester at Low Byrness. Another stretch is held by the Byrness Hotel, which provides visitors' permits.

BATHING

There are no organised facilities. Swimmers will find a number of suitable pools on the North Tyne, the Lewis Burn, the Liddel, and other streams; but as these are fed by cold hill streams they are only pleasant in hot weather. Few pools are suitable for non-swimmers.

CLUBS

The Kielder Working Men's Club is affiliated to the National Association, and offers facilities to members of other affiliated clubs.

MAPS

On the quarter-inch to the mile scale, the whole of the Border National Forest Park, and also the whole of the Northumberland

National Park, are included on Sheet 1 of the Ordnance Survey series, entitled 'The Border'.

On the one-inch to the mile scale, three sheets are required to cover the Forest Park, namely:

Great Britain, No. 76. Carlisle. Shows Newcastleton and Kershope Forests in Liddesdale; south-western areas of Kielder Forest in Tynedale; and western part of Wark Forest (West of Falstone).

Great Britain No. 77. Hexham. Shows south-eastern part of Kielder Forest; and eastern part of Wark Forest; east of Falstone in both cases.

Great Britain No. 70. Jedburgh. Shows Wauchope Forest, Redesdale Forest, and northern portions of Kielder Forest; north of Kielder Castle.

MUSEUMS, ETC.

Northumberland. There are three museums at castles on the Roman Wall, concerned with Roman-British Antiquities, in the care of the Ministry of Works.

That at Chesters, four miles north of Hexham, houses the Clayton Collection of finds from the forts at Chesters, Carrawburgh, House-steads, Greatchesters, and Carvoran. Open from 9 a.m. to 5.30 p.m. in summer (May-September); 9 a.m. to 4 p.m. in winter; opens at 2 p.m. on Sundays. Admission 6d.

That at Corbridge is open from 9 a.m. to 8 p.m. in summer (May-September); 9 a.m. to 4 p.m. in winter; opens at 2 p.m. on Sundays. Admission 6d. Children 3d.

That at Housesteads, six miles north-east of Haltwhistle, is open at similar times and on like terms to Corbridge.

In Newcastle, the zoology and geology of the region are illustrated in the extensive collections of the Hancock Museum, Barras Bridge, which also includes sketches by Thomas Bewick. Admission 6d., children 3d. The Laing Museum and Art Gallery in Higham Place includes a noteworthy collection of landscape paintings, by Henry Burdon Richardson and Charles Richardson, which illustrate the course of the Roman Wall across the county. There is a collection of Bewick's work in the Central Library, which lies adjacent.

Cumberland. There is a comprehensive collection which includes prehistoric Roman, Saxon, and Viking antiquities, and most aspects of natural history, in the Tullie House Museum, Castle Street, Carlisle.

Lanercost Priory, situated 3 miles north-east of Brampton, on a by-road to the north of the main Carlisle-Newcastle road (A69) is a comely ruin built in soft red sandstone. It was founded by Augustinian Canons in 1166 A.D. During the Edwardian wars between

1280 and 1350, it was visited by Edward I, William Wallace, Robert the Bruce, and David II of Scotland, and on the dissolution of the monasteries in 1536 it was granted by Henry VIII to the Dacre family of Naworth Castle. It is now cared for by the Ministry of Works and the church is still used. The secondary road from Lanercost, east to Gilsland, follows a well-preserved stretch of the Roman Wall.

Scotland. The antiquities of the Borders, and particularly those of the Roman period, are well represented in the Scottish National Museum of Antiquities, Queen Street, Edinburgh. Natural History, including geology, is displayed in the Royal Scottish Museum, Chambers Street, Edinburgh.

Hermitage Castle in Liddesdale, and Jedburgh Abbey at Jedburgh, are both under the care of the Ministry of Works, and are open to the public at a small charge.

THE BORDER TODAY

Under an act of James VI of Scotland and I of England, who reigned over both countries from 1603 to 1625, citizens of either country enjoy equal citizenship in each of the two lands. But Scots law and custom are still maintained north of the Border, and English law and custom to the south of it.

> Our native Land—
> Our native Vale—
> A long and last adieu!
> Farewell to bonny Teviotdale
> And Cheviot's mountains blue!

A *Short Guide to the Border Forest Park*, abridged from this one, is published by H.M. Stationery Office at 6d. (postage 3d.)

National Forest Park Guides

Argyll. 3rd Edition. 4s. 0d. (4s. 6d.)
Dean Forest and Wye Valley. 2nd Edition. 5s. 0d. (5s. 6d.)
Glen More (Cairngorms). 2nd Edition. 5s. 0d. (5s. 6d.)
Glen Trool (Galloway). 2nd Edition. 5s. 0d. (5s. 6d.)
National Forest Parks. (Booklet 6). 2s. 6d. (2s. 10d.)
Queen Elizabeth Forest Park Guide. Ben Lomond, Loch Ard
and the Trossachs. 3s. 6d. (4s. 0d.)
Snowdonia. 2nd Edition. 5s. 0d. (5s. 6d.)

Guide Books

Bedgebury, Kent (National Pinetum and Forest Plots). 3rd
Edition. 3s. 6d.
New Forest. 2nd Edition. 5s. 0d. (5s. 6d.)
Cambrian Forests (Mid-Wales). 5s. 0d. (5s. 6d.)
Glamorgan Forests. 5s. 0d. (5s. 6d.)
Westonbirt Arboretum (Glos.). 6d. (9d.)

Printed in England under the authority of Her Majesty's Stationery Office
by ✠Brown Knight & Truscott Ltd., London and Tonbridge

(70171) Wt. 3155 K40 1/62 Gp. 372

NATIONAL FOREST

Glen More.
Cairngorms.

Elgin

Inverness.

Aberdeen

Queen
Elizabeth.
Ben Lomond,
Loch Ard,
The Trossachs.

Dundee

Perth

Oban

Stirling

Argyll.
Cowal.

Edinburgh

Berwick

Glasgow.

Glen Trool
Galloway.

Ayr

Hawick

The Border.

Carlisle.